I0797718

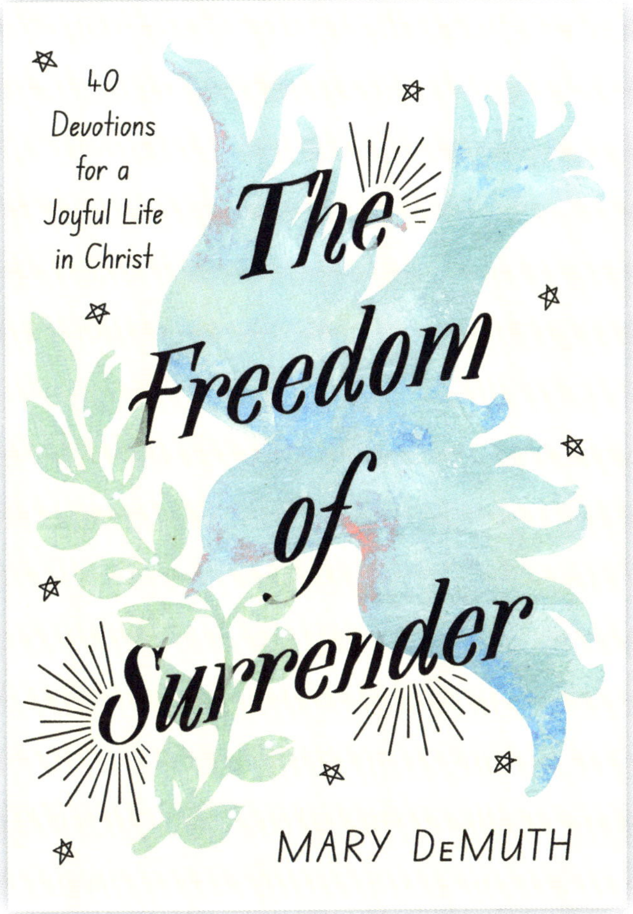

40 Devotions for a Joyful Life in Christ

The Freedom of Surrender

MARY DEMUTH

An imprint of InterVarsity Press
Downers Grove, Illinois

To LaVonda Mason Vestal,

who has learned the painful art of surrender

because she loves Jesus so much.

InterVarsity Press
P.O. Box 1400 | Downers Grove, IL 60515-1426
ivpress.com | email@ivpress.com

InterVarsity Press® is the publishing division of InterVarsity Christian Fellowship/USA®. For more information, visit intervarsity.org.

Interior artwork by Mary DeMuth.

Published in association with Joy Eggerichs Reed of Punchline Agency.

Cover design: Faceout Studio, Molly von Borstel
Interior design: Jeanna Wiggins
Cover images: © Jobalou / DigitalVision Vectors via Getty Images;
© molotovcoketail / DigitalVision Vectors via Getty Images

ISBN 978-1-5140-1134-8 (print) | ISBN 978-1-5140-1135-5 (digital)

Printed in the United States of America ♾

Library of Congress Cataloging-in-Publication Data
Names: DeMuth, Mary E., 1967- author
Title: The freedom of surrender : 40 devotions for a joyful life in Christ / Mary DeMuth.
Description: Downers Grove, IL : IVP, [2025]
Identifiers: LCCN 2025003731 (print) | LCCN 2025003732 (ebook) | ISBN 9781514011348 hardcover | ISBN 9781514011355 ebook
Subjects: LCSH: Christian life–Prayers and devotions
Classification: LCC BV4501.3 .D456 2025 (print) | LCC BV4501.3 (ebook) | DDC 248.4–dc23/eng/20250530
LC record available at https://lccn.loc.gov/2025003731
LC ebook record available at https://lccn.loc.gov/2025003732

30 29 28 27 26 25 | 8 7 6 5 4 3 2 1

CONTENTS

PART FOUR: SURRENDER MY DAILY LIFE

PART FIVE: SURRENDER MY WORRIES

INTRODUCTION

Why Surrendering Is a Necessary Spiritual Practice

IT ALL STARTED THROUGH an acquaintance of mine. Paul is a gifted artist living in another region of Texas. It had been his practice to create a piece of art every day during Lent, which he shared on Instagram. His illustrations stunned me (they were so beautiful), and they helped me understand the Lenten journey in a more nuanced way.

Something stirred in me, a giftedness I had once found superfluous. I have always processed the world through doodling and lettering—so much so that my late grandmother predicted that I would one day have a greeting card line. "You will call it 'Love, Mary Cards,'" she had told me after she opened yet another of my greeting creations. Throughout my growing up years, I was creating with pen, ink, watercolor, and a heart bent to encourage.

But life took over. A degree. A husband. Some kids. And that part of me slowly emaciated over the years. I had forgotten the joy that came when I sat down and created, how time slipped away as I completely forgot the hours. So, with my friend Paul as my inspiration, I created a piece of art every day for Lent. It's been my spiritual practice for a decade now. At first, these were personal pieces, kept solely for me. But eventually I dared to share some of them with my email list to encourage people in their own spiritual journeys. As the years continued, at the behest of a vocal few, I shared the illustrations more widely until I eventually produced a packet of Scripture cards every year, then sold them through my Etsy shop.

I have no formal art training, which, of course, makes me feel highly insecure every time a painting makes its way into the world. But the process of creating has brought me so much joy, and people do seem to be encouraged by the juxtaposition of Scripture and imagery. This last time through my art journey, I combined the theme of surrender with daily illustrations. What if I surrendered something every day of Lent as a spiritual practice and then painted it? And what if I could write a prayer for each surrender? What you're holding in your hands is an expanded iteration of that practice—forty readings on surrender that are a great fit for Lent or any time of year.

Spiritual growth happens after reflecting, considering the sacrifice of Jesus, and preparing our hearts to remember all that he did for us. Though many people give up things (chocolate, for instance) to help them navigate this intentional celebration, what if our practice instead became surrender in every area of life? And what if that practice permeated our lives throughout the year? To surrender is to let go of what we tightly grip, and that kind of purposeful releasing is the precursor to freedom. When we hold fast to control, things, people, outcomes, fame, money, our way of doing things, or expectations, we don't leave room for God to work in those areas. But when we surrender our stress and worries to him, acknowledging that he is wiser and stronger than us, we are off the hook for fixing our lives. In that place of surrender, God does his best work. What better way to celebrate our beautiful Savior than by letting go of the things that have held us back from fully following him?

This forty-day journey of joyful surrender will cover five areas of your life: your inner life, the past, relationships, daily life, and worries. In surrendering in these areas, you are practicing Jesus' counsel in Matthew 16:25: "If you try to hang on to your life, you will lose it. But if you give up your life for my sake, you will save it." There is great benefit in letting go, allowing God to make something beautiful from the current stress you're walking through. Although we benefit from surrender, and joy is mixed into its practice, please know that surrender is not easy. It is a holy practice that hurts because it involves relinquishing control, personally wresting it from ourselves and letting God have the final say. Think of Jesus in the Garden of Gethsemane whose wrestling with the will of God bent toward agony.

To surrender is to let go of knuckled grip. It is a setting aside of control, a holy pause that says I am in need, and God is the great need-filler. While fretting leads to grasping at anything, surrender leads to standing on the firm, solid foundation of God's great love. I know that sounds like a cliché, and I don't mean it to. In this Christian life, though, there are beautiful truths we can anchor ourselves to. There are realities that are more real than the idols we chase. There is hope that replaces the shoddy promises our world doles out like trinkets.

As you surrender, perhaps you could dare to pick up a pen or a paintbrush—just for yourself—to process your letting go on the page. So often our inner journeys toward Jesus are ethereal, but when we create something concrete, we not only seem to experience our journey, but we also have an art piece we can look back on as a reminder of our growth.

My friend Paul demonstrated this possibility to me, that although it's hard for me to call myself an artist, I am like my Father who is the Creator. We are all endowed with a need to create. And often, it is through the act of creation that God uses our own bents to reshape us. Perhaps as you read this book, the Lord will highlight a new calling or hobby or practice that may feel impossible at first but becomes an enriching part of your discipleship journey. Fear often holds us back from trying new things (I know it did for me). But taking a new leap brings its own joy.

My prayer for you is that this surrender journey you're embarking on would deeply transform you. May you point back to this time in your life as the many-moments-strung-together that changed your trajectory—toward more wholeness, hope, and *shalom*.

Day One: I Surrender My Sin

When I illustrated the thorns on this cross, I had them emerge from where the cross touched the ground, revealing the earthly nature of sin and the consequences of the Fall. If you look closely, you'll see that some of the thorns look like people surrendering. Once I finished, I felt like the painting needed more, so I added poppies, a symbol for war veterans, showing us the warfare Jesus endured on the cross.

The beautiful part about surrendering our insides is that Jesus specializes in cleansing us from our sin, the part that messes with our incongruity.

Paul cautions us to "not let any part of your body become an instrument of evil to serve sin. Instead, give yourselves completely to God, for you were dead, but now you have new life. So use your whole body as an instrument to do what is right for the glory of God" (Romans 6:13). Our bodies, our lives, our thoughts are all intended to flourish in this newfound way of living. In surrendering our proclivity to sin, we make way for God's beautiful newness, and we open the door to closeness with him.

The word for sin in Hebrew is *khata*, and the Greek is *hamartia*. While we often think of sin in terms of bad things we do, the simple meaning of these two terms is to fail to make a goal or to miss the mark. In the Bible Project video titled "Khata/Sin," they say, "So in the Bible, sin is a failure to fulfill a goal. But what's the goal? Well, on page one of the Bible, we learn that every human is an image of God, a sacred being who represents the Creator and is worthy of respect. And so in this way of seeing the world, sin is a failure to love God and others by not treating them with the honor they deserve." Put in common terms, to sin is to neglect loving God and others (as Jesus so beautifully reminded us in Matthew 22:37-40).

Seen this way, then, sin is relational in nature. If we choose to push God out of our lives, believing we are happier when we are in control of every outcome, we sin against the triune God who, as Creator, is best qualified to empower us. If we struggle with condemning self-talk, the sin we commit is against ourselves—and we are image bearers of God who should be treated with respect and kindness. Or if we gossip about someone, we are marring the reputation of a fellow human being made in the likeness of God.

Take an inventory of your relationship with God today.

- What are ways I have coped with my life that do not include God?
- Can I identify a habit that is undermining my connection to God?
- Is there something I'm neglecting in pursuing the heart of God?

Understanding that sin is not abstract but relational may help you further explore new areas of surrender. The good news is that the God who loves you and wants you to experience a new, abundant life has provided a remedy for sin through Jesus' perfect sacrifice and resurrection.

Jesus, I surrender my sin to you. Please forgive me for not taking it seriously. Help me internalize what my selfishness and pride have cost you. Thank you for going to the cross to pay for my sin once and for all. Help me understand that when I come to you with my confession, you have forgiven me. I don't want to live in self-condemnation anymore. Amen.

Day Two: I Surrender My Stubbornness

The donkey reminds me of Psalm 81:11-12: "But no, my people wouldn't listen. Israel did not want me around. So I let them follow their own stubborn desires, living according to their own ideas." Although I didn't grow up with donkeys, I did have a particularly stubborn horse growing up who simply had her own agenda. And when she no longer wanted to be ridden, she would buck me off, unmoved by rein, bit, or nudge. May this donkey remind us of the dangers of always getting our own way.

During this season of introspective surrender, ask God to show you different areas of your heart that resist him. To be stubborn is to push against God's path and his counsel, preferring your own way of doing things. I illustrated this by painting an animal known for its stubborn ways.

What does it look like to surrender stubbornness? (Hint: it's not easy!)

First, we admit that God is God, and we are not. He spun the galaxies into existence. He wove us together in our mother's wombs. He sent a flood of judgment upon the sin-scarred earth. He created everything we see. He is strong. He is infinitely wise.

Why is it that we think we can run things better without God? Or we know best how to manage our lives? Perhaps it's pride that fuels us to control things on our own. Or maybe fear—that if we truly surrender, God will disappoint us or lead us down difficult pathways. Our Savior chose the path of surrender. In the Garden of Gethsemane, he famously prayed, "Yet I want your will to be done, not mine" (Luke 22:42). He didn't push God the Father to bend to his desires; he surrendered, instead, to a difficult fate.

God often chooses difficult circumstances to refine us. We seldom grow when all is well—we grow through adversity—so sometimes we are called to surrender to pain as well.

Perhaps our fear fuels stubbornness. We fear what would happen if we let go of our grip on our lives. But consider this: where would we all be if Jesus reversed the prayer in the garden to "Not your will, but mine." That act of stubbornness would have robbed us of the miracle of salvation.

Let's continue our inventory from yesterday by looking at ourselves.

- What current practices or habits have harmed me, my health, or my work?
- In what ways have I struggled with stubbornness?
- Is there an area of healing God is drawing me toward but I am afraid to pursue?

It may be hard to discern when or how we're trying to force God to acquiesce to our plans. We can simply rest in King David's words: "O LORD, you have examined my heart and know everything about me" (Psalm 139:1). He knows you. He loves you. He is a gentle shepherd who reveals your areas of stubbornness. Rest there.

Jesus, I surrender my stubbornness to you. Oh, how I think I know all the things and all the ways to live this life. Often, I sink my heels in, defending myself rather than admitting wrongdoing or error and asking for forgiveness. Help me to be open to new things, to welcome change (even when it scares me), and to transform my personal stubbornness into a deep dependance upon you. Amen.

Day Three: I Surrender My Security

When we are little, we grab for something soft and comforting like the bear in the image—a familiarity of reassurance that helps us when we feel scared, insecure, or alone. I had a stuffed kangaroo that boasted a music box inside. You turned its belly button, and it played a lullaby. I painted a bear/blanket to represent what we run to and to remind us to reach heavenward instead.

We live in an insecure world, and social media feeds it. Everywhere we look, there is someone smarter, more successful, younger, or funnier than us. When we look outwardly at others and use them as a measuring stick, we tend to feel less-than.

But Jesus reminds us of our preciousness. "What is the price of two sparrows—one copper coin? But not a single sparrow can fall to the ground without your Father knowing it. And the very hairs on your head are all numbered. So don't be afraid; you are more valuable to God than a whole flock of sparrows" (Matthew 10:29-31). The good Lord created us utterly extraordinary, with desires, bodies, talents, and hopes that, combined, are truly one in ten billion. There is no other you. And 100 percent you are 100 percent loved by the One who takes care of ordinary sparrows.

It's often easier to turn anywhere but the embrace of God. Why? Because he seems far away, and we need comfort right now. Our insecure hearts find solace in control, substances, addictions, escapes, doom-scrolling, or show binging. There's a supreme difference between the kind of "rest" that numbs us and the kind of sabbath that truly renews us. One places a bandage on an open, seeping wound; the other finds the root cause and brings soul rest.

Our God who loves the sparrows loves to become our security, the place we run when we're overworked, overwhelmed, and overlooked. When life swirls out of control and storms threaten, our God can become the shelter we need—even in relational storms.

Finishing our inventory from day one and two, ask yourself the following questions:

- Is there someone I need to start the journey of forgiveness with?

- Do I need to apologize to someone for my words or actions/inactions?
- Has God prompted me to have a difficult conversation with someone?

Thankfully, God welcomes our angst, even stress involving others. Because he made us to be in relationship with him, he wants to hear from us. Yes, he already knows what we are wrestling with in the middle of the night, awake and afraid, but just like a parent wants to hear the thoughts of their child (even though they know the source of their pain), God wants to interact with us about how we're feeling. To share your insecurity is to bless God with the gift of relationship—it shows him you love him enough to talk to him.

Jesus, I surrender security to you. Or maybe better said, I give you my insecurity and my chasing of that which seems secure. Truly my only security comes when I'm positioning myself upon you, the rock of my life. Forgive me for chasing after people, money, and whatever else that falsely promises security. You are my hiding place. You are my source of refuge. You are the One who will never leave me or forsake me. You are eternal. You never change. Your words stand. You are faithful and true. Secure my heart to yours. Attach me to you, Jesus. Amen.

Day Four: I Surrender My Cynicism

When I think of my own cynicism, I think of how it darkens me, poisoning the way I view the world. Cynicism is abstract, and although I thought a long time about how to portray it concretely, I landed on this imagery to show how pervasive it is, and that often cynicism comes from words imprinted on us when we allow the world's system to permeate us through our media choices.

Cynicism erupts from unmet expectations. We have a vision of what the world should be like and how our lives should pan out, but when circumstances deviate from those cherished ideals, we grow despondent, then angry, then cynical. This is different from bitterness, yet in a nuanced way. Cynicism is expecting everything to fall apart, believing the worst, while bitterness is a state of the heart, a place it remains, a turning inward. Cynicism, once rooted, is hard to weed out of our lives. It darkens even the brightest day. Nursed, it becomes the lens by which we see the world.

James, the brother of Jesus, teaches us a different path. Instead of seeing adverse circumstances as further reason to retreat into ourselves, coddling our cynicism, we can do something different, through the power of the Spirit who so mightily lives within us. "Dear brothers and sisters, when troubles of any kind come your way, consider it an opportunity for great joy. For you know that when your faith is tested, your endurance has a chance to grow. So let it grow, for when your endurance is fully developed, you will be perfect and complete, needing nothing" (James 1:2-4). We can shape-shift those problems to opportunities for joy. Because the truth is we grow best through trials.

As we mature, we learn how to see trials not as enemies but as friends bearing gifts. Look back on your life. When did you grow the most?

- When life perfectly aligned?
- When all your expectations were met?
- When everything went the way you hoped?

Those are moments to remember fondly, but chances are they did not grow you. To escape cynicism is to welcome trials as a discipleship-shaped gift.

We can choose to live expecting the worst, or we can process those very real (and normal) feelings and ask God to change us. Consider the powerful promises Paul writes to the Romans: "We can rejoice, too, when we run into problems and trials, for we know that they help us develop endurance. And endurance develops strength of character, and character strengthens our confident hope of salvation. And this hope will not lead to disappointment. For we know how dearly God loves us, because he has given us the Holy Spirit to fill our hearts with his love" (Romans 5:3-5).

Pain can either drag us into cynicism's abyss, or we can dare to let Jesus replace that with biblical hope.

Jesus, I surrender my cynicism to you. I really don't want to bend toward anticipating the worst—particularly with people, because if I can anticipate the negative I won't be disappointed. Sadly, that's not a very abundant way to live. Please deliver me from cynicism, a quick-to-judge heart, and pessimism. Replace these with hopeful anticipation of what you can do. I want to love others well. I want to have good expectations of others and circumstances. But I can't do that on my own. Hold me when I'm afraid to let go of cynicism. Amen.

Day Five: I Surrender My Apathy

I went for a more obvious depiction here, reminding myself that apathy tends toward lethargy, so I painted how my body is when I'm apathetic, hand on chin, eyes downcast, all while life is being offered in the form of flowers (to no avail). Paul reminds us to be wary of a laissez-faire attitude in Romans 12:11-12: "Never be lazy, but work hard and serve the Lord enthusiastically. Rejoice in our confident hope. Be patient in trouble, and keep on praying." The opposite of apathy is biblical hope.

Apathy is not laziness. It's an abandonment of doing good. This world mitigates against us being a force for good in this world. It is far easier to pretend not to care than to enter the pain of this world and work for justice.

Problems do exist, but we do not work for their sake. Instead, we "serve the Lord enthusiastically" (Romans 12:11). He is our motivation. He is our reason. If we work merely for the sake of good in this world and are persecuted, we may grow weary. But if we work for the sake of the One who created it all, we remain secure because he is secure.

It is an act of defiant joy to rejoice in the unseen hope God provides us supernaturally.

One way to deal with apathy is to remember the meaning of our work. Paul reminds us that our work is not in vain in 1 Corinthians 15:58: "So, my dear brothers and sisters, be strong and immovable. Always work enthusiastically for the Lord, for you know that nothing you do for the Lord is ever useless."

Remembering Hagar from the Old Testament is instructive. She bore Ishmael to Abram, yet twice fled because of Sarai's anger. Utterly alone, she encountered God—even becoming the first person in Scripture to give God a name, El Roi, the God who sees (Genesis 16:13).

As in the case of Hagar who felt unseen and bereft, he is the God who sees us. He sees what we do. He sees what we don't do. He sees us when we feel utterly alone. He takes everything we face all into account. The good news? Our works follow us into eternity.

Apathy festers in isolation. If you're feeling like nothing you do matters, instead of withdrawing, share that fear with a close, safe friend. Chances are they'll encourage you that what you do matters in this world.

Apathy results from a deadened heart, typically after pain upon pain has assaulted us, so be tender with yourself. Retrace your steps. Realize you're normal for feeling that way, then ask God to heal the apathy within.

The truth? You are endowed with worth. Jesus died for you. You were created lovingly by the God of the universe. When you do work that frees others, even when it tires you out, you are doing the work of God. When the world appears to be winning, Christ is still the victor, and all will be well—someday.

Jesus, would you search me for any hidden spots of apathy? And if you find those, help me to face my own lethargy and ask for forgiveness. I confess that I sometimes deaden my heart because it just seems easier that way. That's not a brave or faith-filled way to live. You require holy action in my life. You want me to continue to stretch and grow, but I cannot do that if I sit idly by and let the world win its battles. Give me my fight back, Jesus. Amen.

Day Six: I Surrender My Inner Bully

I painted a woman whose head is topped with a lie she heard at one time, but now she has internalized it as truth and used it as a weapon against herself. "You won't amount to much." I've wielded that lie in a similar manner. I've had to take Paul's words to heart. "My conscience is clear, but that doesn't prove I'm right. It is the Lord himself who will examine me and decide" (1 Corinthians 4:4). It's especially hard when we believe bully words, so I painted her shirt's message to counteract the lie with words of surrender.

We listen to many voices. Shame from the past often shouts louder than kindness in the present. The hollering of social media crowds out the still, quiet voice of God. And often, if we allow it to, our own inner bully can be the most obtrusive of all.

Why is it that we are kinder to strangers than we are to ourselves? Why is it that we can give a hearty nod to loving our neighbors, but when it comes to loving ourselves, we balk? False humility may be in play (where we feel it's "right" to put ourselves down), but perhaps there is more to it?

In case you're curious, here are some examples of what an inner bully might say:

- You never finish a job.
- You're not going to be successful, even if you try.
- You don't deserve love—just look at your appearance!
- You're stupid.
- You'll never overcome the choices of your past.

What happens when those inner bully voices become truth to us? Could it be that they become comfortable? Or better yet, welcomed because they are known? Sometimes dysfunction can be so common in our lives that we mistake it for health. And the constancy of bully thoughts creates a landscape of *this is normal; this is known; this is comfortable; I know how to handle this.*

There is so much more to a rich inner life than constantly policing yourself. Paul hints at this in the 1 Corinthians passage. The Lord keeps us in check. The Holy Spirit within us does the work of conviction. He will not miss anything. He doesn't need us to constantly scrutinize ourselves. And his voice of conviction is not harsh but kindhearted.

Look at the apostle Paul's encouragement to the Corinthian believers in 2 Corinthians 7:10: "For the kind of sorrow God wants us to experience leads us away from sin and results in salvation. There's no regret for that kind of sorrow. But worldly sorrow, which lacks repentance, results in spiritual death." He convicts us without shame and obsessive regret. His voice is clear and helpful.

The safest way to conquer your inner bully is repentance and openness before the Lord who deeply loves you, who is *for* you, and who died and resurrected on your behalf. It's his kindness that leads you toward a life of repentance—a safe place to land, free of condemnation and inner hollering.

Jesus, I surrender my inner bully to you. That bully is loud and fierce, and I often believe what it says. Replace those internal scripts of personal defamation with your kind-hearted encouragement. Help me unlearn those sentences of shame and replace them with your declarations of truth. Remake my thoughts so they represent the gentle sweetness of the Holy Spirit within me. Help me to treat myself as I would treat a very close friend. Amen.

Day Seven: I Surrender My Impatience

As an impatient gardener who runs outside every morning to see if that pesky zucchini seed has sprouted yet, this idea of a seed wondering what's taking so long resonated with me. Growth is not instantaneous. James reminds us of the importance of a farmer's patience. "Dear brothers and sisters, be patient as you wait for the Lord's return. Consider the farmers who patiently wait for the rains in the fall and in the spring. They eagerly look for the valuable harvest to ripen. You, too, must be patient. Take courage, for the coming of the Lord is near" (James 5:7-8).

Gardeners must practice patience. Placing a seed in the ground, then checking on it hours later will produce frustration. It takes time for things to grow and mature, just as it takes us a lifetime to become what God intends. The sanctification journey is marked far more by deliberate slowness than by flashy, fast growth.

But human nature, such that it is, loves instant gratification. It bends toward the shortcut, convenience, and things done exactly the way we want them. Our initial expectations tend toward perfection, so when circumstances don't align perfectly, we give in to impatience.

There is hope, however. A baby is (rightly) impatient for her next meal. Toddlers holler if a want is not addressed. As we move from elementary school ways to teenage life to adulthood, we can grow in our tolerance for things not being the way we want them to be. That's part of growing up.

Patience, according to Paul in Galatians 5, is a fruit of the Spirit of God living within us. It's already a part of our spiritual DNA. So what do we do when we've had an impatient week? How do we let go of impatience and access the patience God so freely gives? The answer involves the heart and intent of this devotional—surrender.

To surrender your impatience is a form of repentance. It's acknowledging that in your own strength, you lean toward tapping your foot, rolling your eyes, and demanding things to be done in your way and timing. Impatience is part of our fleshly nature, yes, but that doesn't mean we have to bow to its demands.

To relinquish impatience is to take inventory of how it has affected our lives. What gifts has impatience given you? Has impatience made you more kind? Has it escalated or de-escalated a heated argument? Has it shortchanged you in the long run? Has the over-practice of it harmed your closest relationships? The truth is, patience improves your life and your relationships, but impatience does the opposite.

Jesus, I surrender my impatience to you. During this time of reflection, I realize how important it is to take inventory of the ways I act that harm me and others. Forgive me for jumping to conclusions in my impatience. Help me to slow my life down enough so that I have space to exercise the patience you so freely offer me. I long for my relationships to flourish, and I understand my lack of patience brings pain there. Looking back over my week, I can see how impatience has soured me. In my own strength, I cannot be patient, but in your strength I can. Please renew my mind. Help me to be patient today, to slow down, and to learn from inconveniences rather than shout at them. Amen.

Day Eight: I Surrender My Anger

All I could think of when I contemplated anger was a volcano spewing its top, so I painted one. Having grown up in the Pacific Northwest, I was alive when Mount St. Helens blew. I still remember the outcome—ash everywhere. One volcano's anger covered an entire state, then the world, in a cloud of ash. This tropical volcano spews magma rather than ash, a sound representation of Proverbs 29:11: "Fools vent their anger, but the wise quietly hold it back."

While it is true we can be angry yet not sin, the nature of anger means we must first surrender it to God so he can temper us. As the proverb says above, wise people know when to hold their tongues. I remember a friend telling me, "I want to be authentic, so that means I say whatever comes to mind in the moment." While that *would* be authentic, if she did not filter her words, she could end up sinning against people. James 1:20 says, "Human anger does not produce the righteousness God desires."

Anger is a strong emotion. Rightly wielded, it can fuel the work for justice where injustice reigns. Wrongly processed, it can not only cause others pain, but if we turn it inward, we can slip into depressive thoughts as well.

To process our anger well, it's important to let it out, but in a safe place. Here are some healthy ways to work through anger:

- Tell God everything that is worrying or bothering you. Say it out loud. This kind of verbalization with the Lord often lets the steam out of the anger engine. Once it's expressed out in the open for God's ears to hear, it loses its punch.
- Write down your angst in a journal or a document on your computer or phone. Before we share it with others, it's helpful to process what we're feeling in a neutral space. (If you don't like writing, try voice to text on your phone, and say it into your device. Then, seeing your words on a page, you'll have a new prophetic distance to look at it more objectively.)
- Once you've done the first two tasks, ask the Lord to show you someone who is safe and wise. Ask permission to talk through your anger with them. (Then listen. Hear their feedback.)

- If there's anger between you and another, prayerfully discern if God is leading you to connect or have a conversation. There is a lot of nuance here. For instance, if the person is abusive, this might not be a good idea. Ask the person you processed the anger with if they feel it would be good to do this step.

Jesus, I surrender my anger to you. Sometimes I can't even keep it straight why I'm angry, and I need you to sift through me to untangle my thoughts. Still, I trust that you can. Send me a safe friend to process my anger. Help me keep a guard over my words so that I don't spew. May my words bring edification in the moment. Even so, Lord, ignite a longing for justice in me as I look at my own anger at injustice in your world. I want to be a catalyst for positive change, properly fueled by righteous anger. But when my anger is not righteous, please help me repent of it, process it, and move forward in love. Amen.

Day Nine: I Surrender My Bitterness

The problem with bitterness is that it erupts from the roots to the treetops. We must dig it out, remembering that God does the kind of inner work that helps us forgive and work through our pain. No leaves decorate this tree. Bad roots equal no growth and, eventually, decay. The author of Hebrews reminds us, "Look after each other so that none of you fails to receive the grace of God. Watch out that no poisonous root of bitterness grows up to trouble you, corrupting many" (Hebrews 12:15).

There's not much we can do about our past, but we can choose to grow beyond what happened back then. To surrender the past is to make peace with it, to trust in God's sovereign ability to make something good out of pain. Our story is not erased but remembered, then surrendered.

No one sets out to be bitter. When we list desired character traits, we don't write *bitterness* on our list. But the insidiousness of trauma, pain, and hurt push against our hearts, and when we spend more time ruminating over the offense rather than continually surrendering it to God, we run into the very real possibility that we're edging toward a bitter heart.

But first, we must explore our grief and provide space to lament. Bitterness comes from *not* addressing a moral injury (typically). We must walk backwards from our bitter thoughts and keep asking questions.

- ☆ Why do I feel this way?
- ☆ What happened to hurt me?
- ☆ Who am I embittered against?
- ☆ Have I grieved?
- ☆ What am I afraid to address?

We live in a broken, sin-haunted world, and we have a soul enemy who delights in trying to destroy us. No wonder we're walking wounded, or bitterness threatens us!

Sometimes we don't know why we're hurting until we write it out, stark on the pages of a journal. For me, that certainly helps, but what furthers my healing is processing it aloud with a loved one. It's then I understand the nature of my pain. To have someone there absorbing it and reflecting back is enlightening. Plus we receive prayer and feedback.

Bitterness need not be an inevitability of your life. To surrender it means you open your heart for lament, then healing, to codify what hurt you. It is right to share your pain with the One who made you rather than ignoring your very real pain in hopes that it will go away. Sadly, punched down pain grows unhindered like cancer, but processed pain has a chance to heal.

The opposite of a bitter heart is a tender one. Hosea 10:12 reminds us, "Plant the good seeds of righteousness, and you will harvest a crop of love. Plow up the hard ground of your hearts, for now is the time to seek the LORD, that he may come and shower righteousness upon you." Hearts can grow hard, but we can seek God and plow hard soil so that it becomes a seedbed of hope.

Jesus, I surrender my bitterness to you. I don't want to live hardhearted anymore. I want to soften. An embittered life only breeds contempt and isolation, so set me free from my pain, my demand to be heard, and my desperation for vindication. I understand not everything will be reconciled here on earth. In the meantime, heal my hurting heart so that it becomes tender and open. Break up the hard soil of my heart, so you can grow something beautiful. Amen.

Day Ten: I Surrender My Past Struggles

This idea didn't come to me immediately so I prayed the Lord would show me an image. An open door with a dark interior came to mind. I drew the doorjamb and door and let it remain white, painted the walls a pale pink, and darkened the interior, representing past struggles. Thankfully, the door is open and beckoning, as is our future. The old is gone; the new awaits.

Paul reassures us, "Anyone who belongs to Christ has become a new person. The old life is gone; a new life has begun!" (2 Corinthians 5:17). It's encouraging to read these straightforward words. But sometimes it's hard to understand what it means that a new life awaits us, particularly when we look backwards and see all the ways we've fallen short (or others have). Remember this: you are human; therefore, you will sin, make mistakes, and do things you regret.

Thankfully, today is a brand-new day, pregnant with potential.

We can remember two things as we look backward. One: God's grace is sufficient, and he loves to bring beauty from ashes. Two: the law of sowing and reaping is also true. God is capable of doing new things with your life, but there are also real-life consequences to past actions. The apostle Paul writes this to the Galatians:

> Don't be misled—you cannot mock the justice of God. You will always harvest what you plant. Those who live only to satisfy their own sinful nature will harvest decay and death from that sinful nature. But those who live to please the Spirit will harvest everlasting life from the Spirit. So let's not get tired of doing what is good. At just the right time we will reap a harvest of blessing if we don't give up. (Galatians 6:7-9)

Yes, our past actions carry weight, but our current good works have a lasting benefit too—a harvest of blessing.

Perhaps one of your past addictions, struggles, or conflicts is haunting you today. You've bought the lie that you ruined everything and grace cannot cover you. Thankfully, you're not that powerful. You cannot thwart the goodness of God through your choices because God always runs a redemptive thread through our tangled stories. The darker threads of sin and past choices, though regrettable, can become the beautiful contrast to the light the Lord brings. The darker the past, the more opportunity for light and growth.

Part of surrendering our past struggles is recognizing our humanness and frailty and letting God know how much we need him every single day. Left to ourselves, we chase after idols, fame, security, relief, and bad relationships. But as we surrender the past, we essentially say, "God, I want to learn from my sins and unhealthy choices. Make those deviations into instructions for wisdom."

When we surrender our past choices, the old truly is gone, and a new life spreads out before us, pristine and beckoning.

Lord, would you reveal the choices I'm ruminating on today—the ones making me sad or holding me back from growth? I understand I cannot change those things. Even though I know your forgiveness is certain, I confess those past sins to you and ask that you would set me free, forgive my sins, and teach me how to live graced today. Thank you that your light shines all the brighter on the canvas of my darker choices. Amen.

Day Eleven: I Surrender the Words Spoken over Me

For this piece, I created the head of the person with actual words spoken over me. Look closely, and you can discern some of those words. I painted it tangled and confusing because I've had a hard time teasing out what was truth or fiction. I had to memorize Psalm 31:20 to retrain my mind, realizing that the "accusing tongues" were my own! "You hide them in the shelter of your presence, safe from those who conspire against them. You shelter them in your presence, far from accusing tongues." I'm still surrendering the words spoken over me, and I'm beginning to see freedom.

Words are powerful and memorable. Sadly, we often remember the negative words spoken over us far more than we recall praise. And those mean words can inform our worth and direction today. So it's time to surrender them. But before we do, a caveat.

While we cringe beneath critical words, we have also harmed others in what we've said. And those memories can hurt just as much because we can't take back those words. James reminds us of our words' power: "Sometimes [the tongue] praises our Lord and Father, and sometimes it curses those who have been made in the image of God. And so blessing and cursing come pouring out of the same mouth. Surely, my brothers and sisters, this is not right!" (James 3:9-10).

While we cannot time travel and magically remove sentences, we can ask the Lord to teach us through that experience. If the person is alive, we can apologize and ask forgiveness. We can ask God to please carry the regret we hold and to offer us grace. Thankfully, he freely offers both grace and forgiveness, but often we forget that truth and cling to shame instead. This is an opportunity to preach the gospel to ourselves, reminding us that God's grace is all sufficient.

Spend time asking God to show you what negative declarations have harmed you today. It may be a parent saying you're in the way or a coach decrying your lack of ability or a friend morphing from companion to betrayer. It's difficult to come up with these phraseologies, so seek a close friend to help. Simply ask, "Is there something I'm believing about myself that's holding me back?" Then trace that belief back to the source.

You are an image bearer of the Almighty God. He loves you. He is for you. You are not the sum of the words spoken over you. You no longer need to carry those stories as if they are truth. Place them firmly in the fable category instead. They are fiction that is informing the way you feel and act today. Let them go. Pour them out to the One who loves you well.

Jesus, I surrender those words spoken over me. They still sting, still try to define me. But I no longer want to be shaped by those stories anymore. Overwhelm me with your love so that the lies shrink into nothingness. The truth is you love me. You cheerlead me. You created me. I matter. I will amount to something because you have given me life and purpose. I am not insignificant. I am wanted, valued, and cared for. May those words be megaphoned in me, and may the lies spoken over me whisper into silence, I pray. Amen.

Day Twelve: I Surrender My Difficult Memories

I'm not great at painting people, so I prayed about these limitations, then asked God for an image or metaphor to represent the jumble of memories we carry. This idea of an interwoven series of hearts, a bit tangled and clearly in the past, came to mind. Such a simple idea, really. Our difficult memories can be tangled, but it's where our own hearts originated, and though it's hard to see it, how we grew up shaped us into who we are today. We are separate from those memories but tethered too. And, thankfully, God works through the entirety of our life, represented by the continual string.

We all have things we grieve about our past. Expectations unmet. Pains experienced. Words said or unsaid. Events that took our breath away. No human family is perfect, nor do they perfectly navigate this sin-influenced life. The psalmist clearly communicates the angst we may feel if we had caregivers who hurt us but reminds us of the good parenthood of God. "Even if my father and mother abandon me, the LORD will hold me close" (Psalm 27:10).

Today, journal about the memories you carry that are difficult, noting what comes to mind (don't feel like you must remember everything), as well as comforting or poignant ones. The Lord is a gentle healer; he is kindhearted when he soothes our wounds and hears our cries. He doesn't barge in. He opens the door and waits for us to walk through. He doesn't give us everything at once, otherwise we would be completely overwhelmed.

The Lord will help you recall a single painful memory to surrender. As a latchkey kid, I fidgeted with my key, looking over my shoulder, convinced someone was following me home from elementary school. And the moment I opened the creaky back door, I locked it and called my grandmother who would listen to me and make sure I was safe. The memory is divergent—both the fear of being alone and the comforting voice of my grandmother.

Memory of the past is tinged both ways, isn't it? To surrender the bad, I have an opportunity to thank the Lord for the good, and perhaps this will be your experience today. For the longest time, in retrospect I could not recall one good memory. The negative ones had a louder bite, and they crowded out any good ones. After a while, the good memories started to surface—an indication I was healing.

When surrendering, be aware that questions may arise that require some working through. For instance, you might have questions: *Why didn't I experience rescue?* or *Why did God allow that trauma?* or *Did God love me in the midst of that horrible situation?* Don't be afraid to voice those honest questions.

Lord, instead of trying to recall all my difficult memories, will you help me recall a memory that is holding me back? I want to continually surrender to you—even the difficult parts of my story. I lay down the pain I experienced. I give you my honest questions. I surrender my expectations (both met and unmet), and I ask you to help me reframe any pain into a new way of seeing things. Please be near me as I look backward. Amen.

Day Thirteen: I Surrender My Trauma

One of the results of trauma is how it causes us to ruminate. Initially I created a scribbled design on this unfaced woman, but as I thought about it, I scrapped that painting and added flowers instead. Why? Because even though trauma is terrible and hard, the beauty that emerges from it is profound. Perhaps that picture brings you hope? What a beautiful thought that "the Lord is close to the brokenhearted; he rescues those whose spirits are crushed" (Psalm 34:18).

Trauma never used to be talked about, but today it's a term that's common in our vernacular. Trauma happens when we've experienced an incident or a series of difficulties that feel (or are) life threatening or emotionally devastating. The consequences of trauma affect all of us—our souls, bodies, emotions, relationships, and our connection to God. There are varying degrees of trauma, some long term (like childhood neglect), some short term (like a car accident). But any sort of trauma results in an injury—one that is difficult to recover from.

To surrender trauma, you must go back to that place of pain and be willing to let God into the intricacies of that incident. This is not easy, and often involves the help of a trauma-informed counselor, particularly if you are prone to being triggered by that trauma.

One helpful way to process past pain that may feel safer is to write it out for only you (and the Lord) to see. Give yourself permission to write down what happened, as much or as little detail as you feel you can write. The Lord already knows that you're upset about that past event, and his shoulders are strong enough to carry your anger, doubts, confusion, and questions. He can "take" your complex emotions, bewilderment, and even ambivalence.

The common illustration of submerging a beach ball at a pool is helpful. It's not hard to submerge it, but because it's full of air, it inevitably pops up. To tell your story of pain is to take the air out of the beach ball. Then it is easier to submerge. We wrongly think that avoidance means we've dealt with something, but facing it with others not only disempowers the weight of our pain story, but it *empowers* us to finally let go.

An important note: trauma is the "gift" that keeps on giving. It is insidious, and even though we feel we've completely dealt with it, new layers of it can trigger us out of the blue. It's at those times we're tempted to think we've done no surrendering and had zero growth. Not true. The healing journey is layered and complex, and we will not be fully delivered from 100 percent of our past pain until we see Jesus face to face. Don't allow a triggering event to lie to you. You have been healing. You are healing. You will be healing.

Jesus, I surrender my trauma to you. I understand how complex it is, but I'm also tired of the triggering and the slow way the healing journey works. Please heal those parts of me I cannot heal. Show me counselors who are helpful and trauma informed. Thank you for being a wonderful counselor. Show me where I've allowed trauma to define me, where I haven't pursued healing because trauma feels more normal. Instead, Lord, I want to get well. Show me a pathway forward. Shine a light through this darkened path. Amen.

Day Fourteen: I Surrender My Healing Journey

The journey through healing is arduous, so I created my own "healing island" pathway with the forest of fortitude, castle of confusion, lake of loneliness, river of restlessness, mountains of mourning, beachhead of bewilderment, and, finally, the garden of gratitude. Since I've walked such a journey, it wasn't hard to uncover these "places" I've trod. There's also the importance of an island, which can feel quite isolating. In my own healing journey, I've often felt alone.

The paralyzed man remained unhealed for nearly four decades, and we encounter his story just before Jesus asks him an important question. "One of the men lying there had been sick for thirty-eight years. When Jesus saw him and knew he had been ill for a long time, he asked him, 'Would you like to get well?'" (John 5:5-6). Jesus interacts with him on the sabbath at the Sheep Gate, where crowds of broken people gathered around the pool of Bethesda, hoping for a cure.

Jesus' question is curious. Wouldn't anyone *want* to get well? Interestingly, the man never answers the question. Instead he says, "I can't sir . . . for I have no one to put me into the pool when the water bubbles up. Someone else always gets there ahead of me" (John 5:7). He's referring to something akin to the "stirring of the waters" where, if you were lucky, you'd be the first in the water and be healed when it churned (or an angel visited it). Instead of answering, the man gives an excuse—quite a logical one at that.

Even though the man didn't respond, Jesus still chose to heal him by commanding him to rise, pick up his mat, and walk. In an instant, he moved from lame to ambulatory. And then he spent the rest of his life walking out that healing.

Jesus asks you a similar question: Do you *want* to get well? Do you want to be set free from what happened to you yesterday, the year before, or farther back? To heal means unfamiliarity—facing the kind of scary adventure that is unpredictable.

To surrender the healing journey is to let go of the expectations for how the pathway will look. It means looking realistically at what happened back then, then giving God permission to do something new.

The Lord knows what we need. He knows the intricacies of what we went through when we were hurt. He sees the whole of our pathway and leads us gently from grace to grace. He is best equipped to uncover what is best for the moment, and he knows the broken parts of us that need addressing in his perfect timing. What a good God we serve!

Know this: Jesus wants to heal you. He wants to move you from unable to able, from little strength to greater strength. He loves you and knows what is best for you. Even if you can't answer the question about wanting to get well, he chooses to heal you.

Lord, I surrender my healing journey to you. I admit that sometimes I'm scared to open myself up to you, and there have been times when I've prescribed my healing journey to you rather than waited on your perfect timing. I praise you for taking me this far. And I anticipate with joy the ways you are going to set me free. Thank you for being a God who loves to heal his children. Amen.

Day Fifteen: I Surrender My Grief

The picture God gave me: an armoire of coats, though if you push through them, you wouldn't reach Narnia. Instead you'd encounter grief, something that is often closeted and shoved out of view. This armoire's door is open, and inside are coats labeled with the classic stages of grief: denial, anger, bargaining, depression, and acceptance. I've worn every coat; have you? Did you know there's a blessing reserved for grievers? Jesus famously said in the Sermon on the Mount, "God blesses those who mourn, for they will be comforted" (Matthew 5:4).

Grief marks the life of everyone. We see the grief of banishment, of losing a child, of sin ruining everything in the book of Genesis. And because of humankind's fall, death haunts us all.

Grieving is something we learn how to do—much like the sanctification journey we take. We may be slow at it when we first practice it, only to grow in our ability to recognize, carry, and process it. In short, it's a muscle we nurture, though we stumble forward.

Grief is an insistent beast. It must be noticed. If denied, it festers, then turns into numbness or depression. It cannot be processed well in isolation. It must be borne.

Thankfully, we have a picture from the prophet Isaiah whose telescoping words point to the One who would gladly carry our grief. "Yet it was our weaknesses he carried; it was our sorrows that weighed him down. And we thought his troubles were a punishment from God, a punishment for his own sins!" (Isaiah 53:4). Friend, he carries you in your grief.

To surrender our grief is to first name it. Looking back, can you recall the times you wept? Or if you weren't prone to crying, can you remember a time you "pulled yourself up by your bootstraps" to get over a period of sadness? If those times have not been properly given to Jesus, chances are you're still affected by that grief today.

That doesn't mean that once you surrender your grief it won't revisit you. Grief is cyclical; it comes back around. In those times of remembrance, you simply have another opportunity to ask Jesus to bear that grief for you.

Grief comes in many forms, not just the death of a loved one. Consider these aspects of grief:

- death of a dream
- when a friend abandons the relationship
- when a church has harmed you
- when you've been fired or let go
- when your expectations have been dashed
- when you experience an unexpected financial downturn
- when you lose an opportunity (and have no ability to open that door again)
- when your health breaks
- when a child rebels
- when you nurse a regret

In surrendering, you're simply handing grief over to the One who loves to bear every pain you encounter, every loss you've experienced. He is faithful to bear it. He is kindhearted and willing. You are not bothering him with your grief.

Jesus, I surrender my grief to you. It's knotted and tangled and sometimes I can't even articulate why I'm so sad. But you know me from the inside out. You know my internal landscape. You know best how to bear the weight of this grief I've carried for far too long. I want to move through it, Lord. Send me a friend or safe person who can listen to my grief story, dignify it, and pray me through it. Thank you for carrying your followers' grief. Amen.

Day Sixteen: I Surrender My Regrets

Initially I painted the messy-bun woman with her tangled, regretful thoughts in a cloud to symbolize the kind of dreary hold regret holds over us. But then I "ruined" the painting with one orange flower—it's like it had to be there—and then I painted a beautiful future in the form of lively vines. It reminds me of Isaiah 43:18-19: "But forget all that—it is nothing compared to what I am going to do. For I am about to do something new. See, I have already begun! Do you not see it? I will make a pathway through the wilderness. I will create rivers in the dry wasteland." Life calls us forth. Regret may darken our past, but beauty awaits.

The past is a tricky thing.

When we overthink the actions and words we regret, we crowd out what God wants to do in, through, and for us currently. It's unfruitful to dwell in the land of regret because it causes such a backward glance that we no longer can anticipate the future well.

Oswald Chambers in *My Utmost for His Highest* has a beautiful quote that may empower you as you surrender your regret. "Let the past sleep, but let it sleep on the bosom of Christ, and go out into the irresistible future with him." We must let the past sleep. We cannot repair it. But we can surrender so that Christ holds it. When we're mired in the past, we become blind to the "irresistible future."

You cannot atone for your past. You cannot remake it. But you can surrender, asking God to reframe your mistakes and sins in light of his ever-expanding kingdom. Remember, nothing takes God by surprise. Your wrong action cannot thwart the plans of God. He is always working behind the broken scenes of our lives, creating beauty from ashes.

Here are some regrets to consider surrendering.

- following someone else's plan for your life rather than what fit you best
- overworking
- not expressing your feelings when you wanted to
- withholding good things (sins of omission)
- letting go of a relationship that you miss
- making financial mistakes
- violating a clear command of Scripture
- bullying someone
- allowing bullying to prevail

- numbing yourself through scrolling, addictive behavior, food, or substances
- worrying too much about what others thought of you
- failing to take risks
- resisting a new hobby you've been meaning to try
- making decisions based on fear rather than faith
- ruminating on the words you can't take back
- embittering your heart
- living with unforgiveness
- making unhealthy lifestyle choices
- living apart from the Lord, rebelling and doing things your own way

You are not defined by your regret—the Lord defines you through the lens of his affection for you. He has listened to your surrender. He has forgiven what needs to be pardoned. And he has given you an utterly irresistible future.

Lord, I don't want to live in the land of regret. But to do that, I need to surrender the regrets that come to mind today. Please reveal the most insidious ones so I can share them with you and be set free. Remind me that as I surrender, you are always working things out in your perfect plan. Thank you for today's verse that reminds me to face forward, that you are bringing an unbelievable future my way. Untangle me from the past so I can be alert and ready to welcome your new plan, I pray. Amen.

Day Seventeen: I Surrender That Broken Relationship

I wanted to portray conflict between two parties, to represent any gender, so you could relate to them. In the tangled words of conflict, I painted a heart to show the possibility of reconciliation. The apostle Paul alludes to this when he writes to the Philippian believers: "Now I appeal to Euodia and Syntyche. Please, because you belong to the Lord, settle your disagreement. And I ask you, my true partner, to help these two women, for they worked hard with me in telling others the Good News. They worked along with Clement and the rest of my co-workers, whose names are written in the Book of Life" (Philippians 4:2-3).

Broken relationships are inevitable. When two people interact, they bring their baggage, worries, insecurities, and fears into the center of that relational space. There's bound to be heartache.

What can we do? First, we examine our hearts. Jesus reminds us that we cannot see clearly to take a splinter from someone's eye if we have a log in our own (see Matthew 7:5). Asking the Lord to search our hearts is a solid first step toward potential reconciliation. This is not easy, to be sure, and there are times conflict cannot be avoided, remedied, or reconciled. Bearing the weight of conflict is one of the most difficult surrenders we encounter because we realize we truly have so little control over the outcome.

Next, we may need the help of another. Paul, in Philippians 4:2-3, recommends reconciliation—but with help. In the disagreement between Euodia and Syntyche, the two had allowed discord to become the final say, so Paul reminds the leaders to step in. Sometimes there is so much pain we need people outside the disagreement to filter us and bring clarity.

Last, we must remind ourselves that there's only so much we can do. We can be responsible for our own side of things, but if the other person does not want to reconcile, all we can do is pray. Also, it's important to note that some people are dangerous, and their presence in our lives becomes injurious, whether that's intentional on their part or the result of a mental health struggle, for example. Staying in harmful relationships only serves to harm us.

None of us like the dynamics of an unfinished story, particularly a relational one. We love to have endings to conflicts. But this side of the new heaven and the new earth we cannot expect that kind of "end" to happen. Certainly we can pray for it, but because of sin permeating this world (both in us and in others), we may not achieve the harmony we long for.

Surrendering to the Lord (who will not abandon us) becomes a powerful way to salve a relational wound. A relational wound requires a relational cure—and Jesus loves to carry us when we're hurt by others. He understands.

Jesus, I surrender that broken relationship to you. My hope is that the relationship will get better, but I can't see my way toward that end. It feels irrevocably messed up. So all I can do is let go of the outcomes I've longed for, ask you to search my heart for how I may have contributed to the relationship's downfall, and trust you for next steps. In your time, please bring reconciliation, but if that's not possible, would you heal my heart from the aftermath of the pain? Amen.

Day Eighteen: I Surrender My Relational Failure

We talk to each other with different agendas, and we may even be using the same words, but our internal definitions differ. I prayed about it, and this idea of apples and oranges came to me representing just how hard it is to communicate, after I saw a similar painting of two artists. I painted these people looking toward each other but still not understanding what the other was saying. It takes a great deal of intentional listening to truly discern another's perspective.

We tend to map those times when we failed in a relationship. As I reflect, it's often my insecurity, fear, or immaturity that fueled my mistreatment of others. Oh, how I wish I could rewind the clock and reverse what I said!

But we cannot take back our words.

What we can do is surrender our regret to the One who can bring redemption even from our verbal missteps. God is in the business of turning words and worlds around. When we remain despondent about our past sin, we tend to deify our word choices. The truth is we cannot ultimately thwart God's long-term plan for another, though our words do have consequences.

Jesus helps us when we're living in that regret. He reminds us to proactively approach our friend, though that is difficult. Return involves surrender, particularly if we fear conflict. He said, "So if you are presenting a sacrifice at the altar in the Temple and you suddenly remember that someone has something against you, leave your sacrifice there at the altar. Go and be reconciled to that person. Then come and offer your sacrifice to God" (Matthew 5:23-24). Reconciliation requires an in-person conversation.

Whether the relational failure involves only them (it rarely does) or only you (same), we still have the onus to do what only we can.

We can lament the words we regret.

If we have hurt another, causing a relational failure, we can ask for forgiveness without expecting an apology in reply.

We can trust that God best sees the entirety of the mess between us.

What do we do as we live in the tension of an unfinished relationship story?

We can humble ourselves before God, asking him to please help us change what led to our unkind words in the first place.

We can ask God to give us insight into the pain our words have caused the other.

We can gain counsel from a seasoned friend or wise counselor, unpacking what happened and what we could have said differently.

Another thing: we cannot prescribe another's forgiveness pathway. Their journey may take some time, even after an apology. You may have to demonstrate your kindness and patience over years before they can view you as safe. There are consequences to our words, after all.

Last, we can rest in the sovereign ways of God, trusting that he can do the work that we cannot, bridging the wide gap, and softening a heart.

Jesus, I surrender my relational failure to you. I spend so much time reliving that past conversation that it's become a dark cloud over my soul. Show me how to repent. Teach me how to apologize. Wash me clean. Teach me why I've resorted to sinning against another, and help me to be wiser and more patient with my speech next time. I give you the timetable of reconciliation. I pray you would heal the person I harmed. Give them the ability to forgive. Cause them to flourish where they are. Restore that relationship in your perfect timing. Amen.

Day Nineteen: I Surrender when I Disappointed Someone

When I disappoint someone, I feel the chasm widen between us, so I painted a bridge, broken in its belly, to symbolize the rift in relationship. To portray the love missed between, I painted hearts that descend toward the water below because it best portrays the pain we feel after disappointing a friend or family member. But there is much we can do. Our actions, coupled with the grace of Jesus, help us repair that breach.

Life and relationships the way they are, you've probably experienced many nuances in the aftermath of disappointing someone. Sometimes we harm people in the way we act toward them, or perhaps we have deceived them, or maybe we've let jealousy divide us. Amid a difficult moment, we don't always respond with grace (and build a relational bridge).

But there are other issues with disappointment. Sometimes we possess no malicious intent, and no matter what we do, we discover we've disappointed someone. And even if we apologize for our actions, another person may choose to live in that disappointment.

So surrender looks differently in those two instances.

In the first instance, if we have hurt someone, we have the joyful (and painful) opportunity to apologize and ask for forgiveness, making our way back toward our loved one. We always can choose to keep a short account. Of course, how they respond is up to them (will they build their side of the bridge?), but as much as it depends on us, we can freely confess our painful actions. There is no safer place than the place of confession and repentance.

In the second instance, while you still have an opportunity to talk through what happened, if the person chooses to remain disappointed in you, what can you do? You cannot force them to love you back. It may take time for them to trust you again. They may even remain disappointed, something you cannot control. Or maybe through the interaction, you've realized they've held expectations of you that are unfair or unrealistic.

God designed us for bridge-building reconciliation—it's a ministry we've been given. "For God was in Christ, reconciling the world to himself, no longer counting people's sins against them. And he gave us this wonderful message of reconciliation" (2 Corinthians 5:19). Although that verse references the very important task of helping people reconcile to God, God also longs for us to be connected to each other. The whole of the New Testament commandments is simply this: to love God and love others.

When you disappoint someone through your actions, and you've done everything you can do to make it right (yet they remain disappointed), surrender is the most beautiful place to land. Placing another in the hands of the One who loves them well is a spiritual act, saying that God knows best how to do what only he can do.

Jesus, I surrender when I've disappointed someone. I wish I could take back what happened, but I can't. I pray you would help that person forgive me and offer me grace, more for their sake than mine. I pray I'd learn something from this interaction, how to be more attentive, kind, and patient. And yet, Lord, I'm so grateful that you use failures to build my character. You don't heap shame upon me. You love me right now, even when I've disappointed someone else and myself. Help me to rest in your true and gentle forgiveness today, I pray. Amen.

Day Twenty: I Surrender My Desire for That Person to Change

I chose to illustrate this prayer with a cactus, reminding myself that I can be prickly, as can other people. And we cannot fundamentally change the nature of a plant. But we can exercise caution around people who are hurting others (and themselves). And we can still nurture the other. I'm often indebted to the wisdom of Jeremiah when he recounts the nature of all our hearts. "The human heart is the most deceitful of all things, and desperately wicked. Who really knows how bad it is? But I, the Lord, search all hearts and examine secret motives. I give all people their due rewards, according to what their actions deserve" (Jeremiah 17:9-10).

It's normal to long for healing for another. Having that desire hints at hope for restoration. But when we tie our own happiness to the actions of others, and our sadness rises and falls on their antics, it's time to surrender those desires.

Jeremiah's words remind us that we can't even really discern our own hearts, let alone another's. It is only God who can rightly know, then help, the other. He can understand motivations, the many layers of desire, and why we do things. So, to surrender another is to surrender them to God's capable care.

The more mature we grow as Christ followers, the more we realize even changing ourselves is a cooperative effort between our will and our Father's capabilities. And since we cannot change the will of another, the only way to have freedom from the results of another's actions is to remember that God holds them, knows them, and has a beautiful, them-shaped journey to walk.

This is especially difficult when the other person is harming others, us, or themselves. We want to rush in and rescue, helping them see the destructiveness of their ways, but even if we could convince them, they still must decide to seek their own help. We cannot be a surrogate to their will. They must *want* to be free.

So what are we to do? We can certainly pray. I have often petitioned God, "Lord, help my friend to want to long for change. Give them the desire to reach for you."

We can also listen to them, asking clarifying questions, and offering help if or when they ask for it.

We can create boundaries to protect ourselves from their destructive choices.

We can seek wisdom from someone outside the circle of the relationship to better understand how to love our friend or family member well.

We can ask the Lord to be our joy, that even if/when our person hurts us or others or themselves, we can still find bedrock satisfaction on the steadfastness of God.

Jesus, I surrender my desire for that person to change. Help me not to hinge my happiness on their decisions or the state of our relationship. I don't want that other person to be my idol. Please forgive me. Teach me how to intercede in prayer for them, but also help me to understand I cannot change another's life. I choose to remember that the only person I can bring change to is me and then only with the help of your Spirit living within me. Untether my happiness from the decisions of others, I pray. Amen.

Day Twenty-One: I Surrender My Friendships

Birds love to sing from high up, on tree branches or power lines. Wherever they are, they're typically not alone, which is why I used this imagery to convey a surrendered friendship. Sometimes our friends stay with us on the wire; other times they fly away to new adventures. In either case, they are still fundamentally birds who are noticed and cared for by their Creator.

I used to falsely believe that every one of my friends had to remain in the same locale for the rest of my life. I didn't give space for changing dynamics, moving, or different stages of life. Once a friend, always a friend—that was my motto.

But in this transitory world, we cannot hang our hats on this kind of desire. Why? Because friendships shift, our perspectives change, and people move around. Friendships wax and wane. Sometimes they falter. And other times, they beautifully resurrect. Some cannot be repaired this side of eternity.

So how do we hold our friendships loosely yet still pursue the people God has placed in our lives? We can surrender them to the Lord, letting him order our relationships. We can ask the Lord who to pursue. We can become deeply curious about the friends God has peopled our lives with. And we can ask the Lord to open our eyes to new possible friendships. They do deeply benefit our lives, after all. We need them. Proverbs 27:9 reminds us, "The heartfelt counsel of a friend is as sweet as perfume and incense."

Friends scent our lives. And to have a passel of good, solid friends, we must remember the role we play in it. To have good friends is to be a good friend. Perhaps the best way to cultivate deep and lasting relationships is to further develop our friendship capabilities.

A good friend

- listens first and asks open-ended questions.
- rejoices when a friend is happy.
- cries when a friend is in distress.
- looks for ways to serve a friend.
- is attune to the needs of a friend.
- tangibly meets the needs of a friend.

- offers advice when it is solicited.
- prays for their friends.
- has shared interests, typically.
- is long-suffering, even in dry times.
- gives sacrificially.
- stops their lives for the sake of the need of another.

Our friendships shift throughout our lives, but one thing does not shift—God's friendship with us. His relationship with us empowers us to be dedicated, to know our worth, and to realize when we must let go.

Jesus, I surrender my friendships to you. It's hard for me to say goodbye to some. Show me when to let go and when to hold on. Keep my heart open for new relationships you send my way. I don't want to close off my heart in the aftermath of a broken friendship. Would you repair what's been broken? Would you give me insight into myself so I can be an empathetic, encouraging friend for others? Thank you that even if my friends move or move on, you are always my best friend, and you will never leave me or betray me. Amen.

Day Twenty-Two: I Surrender My Need to Be Right

We live in a culture where everyone needs to be right. We holler at each other our rightness, emphasizing our logic and the other's misguidedness. We exemplify the first part of this verse, but shy away from the latter. "Pride leads to disgrace, but with humility comes wisdom" (Proverbs 11:2). So, I decided to emphasize (with exclamation points!) our penchant for wanting our way, longing for our opinions to triumph over another's.

Needing to be right is a character trait of human nature, and it's also an indication that we are battling insecurity. When we are insecure, we have an insatiable need to be right—and praised for our rightness.

But, we cannot possibly always be right.

Let that sink in for a moment.

If you look back on your life even ten years ago, chances are you wouldn't agree with younger you on a variety of topics. Why? Because the longer you live, the more wisdom you acquire. What often seemed quite easily black and white grays with age, and nuance comes dancing into your opinions. It's not that we become wishy-washy the older we get; it's that we realize how little we know.

Curiosity is one of the most beautiful relational traits. Instead of jumping to judgment, growth comes instead when our fallback becomes curiosity. Pride would say "I am right" at any cost, which could threaten relational health. Humility, coupled with inquisitiveness, opens the door for disagreement, but with welcoming grace.

If you feel you need to be right to feel okay, it may mean you are basing your worth on your rightness, not on the foundational truth of the rightness of God. Or you may fear that if someone disagrees with you, they are disagreeing with God (so it is your onus to help them). In both cases, we need the Lord, either to fill us up or to defend his own reputation. His are the only opinions and ideas that are perfect. His love for us is the bedrock truth we can stand on when people's opinions of us are fickle or unfair. God has not called us to "perfect" opinions—he has welcomed us to his perfect self.

We see this in the Gospels, where the religious leaders codified all the right ways to believe and live. These extraneous "commands" straightjacketed people who wanted to follow God because they could never measure up to the minutiae. We are not meant to acquire right opinions as much as pursue a covenantal relationship with the God who loves us, knows us, and sacrificed himself for us.

With God's love as our foundation, we shift from a codex of rules to a warm interaction with the One who is always right. Nestled into the beauty of that truth, the insatiable need to prove our worth by our perfect rightness pales in comparison to the peace that comes from simply being loved.

Jesus, I surrender my need to be right. Help me dig beneath the surface of that need, unearthing why I must be right. I know it affects my relationships. Just as I have grace for me ten years ago when my opinions differed, help me have that same grace for others. Reorient my heart away from rules and toward relationship with you. You are my true north, my foundation, my savior. You alone are right. I surrender my pride that makes me need to be right. Instead, Lord, would you replace that with the humility your Spirit so freely offers? Amen.

Day Twenty-Three: I Surrender My Relational Hopes

Having a hot beverage with a friend indicates the potential a relationship has. I often meet people I've never met before over a cup of tea. There's so much potential in that first sip, and I love the opportunity to become curious about another's story. There's so much potential for love, just as Jesus declared. "This is my commandment: Love each other in the same way I have loved you. There is no greater love than to lay down one's life for one's friends" (John 15:12-13). Perhaps your next cup will be the beginning of a promising friendship!

Every day we have aspirations, expectations, and desires—and many of those traits relate to the relationships in our lives. We hope for reconciliation. We pray for understanding. We try to mitigate against bitterness and unforgiveness. We lament those who stray from Jesus. We rehash old relational wounds. We hurt when another hurts, not knowing how to help them.

Part of surrendering our hopes in friendships, family relationships, and church connections—and even acquaintances—is to understand the *imago Dei*, the image of God in each person we long to know. Everyone holds a treasure within them, though sometimes it's hard to find that when there's discord or pain living between you.

John 15:12-13 reminds us of the sacrificial nature of love for others—to commit ourselves to service rather than demanding to be served. Jesus told his disciples, "For even the Son of Man came not to be served but to serve others and to give his life as a ransom for many" (Mark 10:45). You may say, *well that's all good, but I'm not Jesus*. That's true. But you have his Spirit living within you, and he empowers you to love the unlovely, to serve the broken, to practice empathy with the hurting. Why? Because he loves the person you're struggling with far more than you do, and he loves to love them.

Sometimes our relational hopes sideline us. We live in an unfinished story, longing for the denouement of a repaired friendship. In that liminal space between what is and what we long for, there is space for lament. To work through what isn't in your relationships, it's entirely permissible to grieve what is.

Prayer is the honest link between what you're experiencing now and what you hope to happen in that tattered place. God knows your heart. He knows your sadness and longing and questions about those people you're hurting about. Why not process that with him today in a surrendered prayer?

Jesus, I have so many hopes for so many relationships, but some of them have not materialized the way I envisioned them. So right now, I process that pain with you. Please help me not become callous. I don't want to give in to discouragement so much that I stop praying. Instead, instill in me the kind of hope that keeps me joyful—not wishful thinking, but a solid trust in your ability to change another's life. And as I wait for that friendship to shift and change, help me to look at the log in my own eye. Bring me to yourself. Convict me of my sin. Clean my heart and motives clear out. I surrender that person right now, but as I do, I surrender myself. Amen.

Day Twenty-Four: I Surrender My Current Family

I love the idea of a current, how it moves in and through itself, wave upon wave. Although I intended the word ***current*** *to mean the people who are around us right now, there's also a fluidity of relationships we often experience. And no matter who our family is right now, we always can love them well.*

Paul wrote this love ethic to the Corinthian church. Contrary to popular usage, his instructions are not merely for married people, but for the whole family of God. "Love is patient and kind. Love is not jealous or boastful or proud or rude. It does not demand its own way. It is not irritable, and it keeps no record of being wronged. It does not rejoice about injustice but rejoices whenever the truth wins out. Love never gives up, never loses faith, is always hopeful, and endures through every circumstance" (1 Corinthians 13:4-7).

Often, we are kinder to outsiders than we are to those peopling our lives. Paul wrote the famous verses above to an infighting congregation (much like a family). He emphasized the multifaceted traits of love, fleshing them out to remind us how to love.

You could replace love with the name of Jesus. Jesus is patient and kind—and as his followers, we are to emulate that as well. What better place to practice these traits than in the soil of our families? What would it look like if we truly believed and lived out these verses in the context of difficult family relationships?

We may use manipulation, coercion, and nagging to impose our story upon our families, rather than letting God write their stories. Sadly, we cannot prevent another from meandering down a path we would rather them not.

So what *can* we do? We can ask God to teach us patience and kindness as we wait for him to work in our loved one's life. We can choose to respond without rudeness, pride, or judgment. We can set aside our will for their lives and listen more than we prescribe. We can forgive. We can shout our praise heavenward when our family member makes a good choice. We can endure, practicing the art of steadfast patience (as our God does toward us). We can cling to biblical hope even when circumstances mitigate against it.

To love that way is a part of the surrender.

I used to think I could find perfect harmony in my relationships on earth, and I had to strive to find it. But just when all family relationships seemed good, someone (or me) would upset the balance. There's never a moment when everyone lives in harmony; drama seems to lurk everywhere. So, we must surrender that idea that an ideal will happen exactly the way we want or plan it to, letting God orchestrate the story of each of our family members.

Jesus, I surrender my family to you. There are complicated relationships represented there and sweet, connected ones too. Would you help me weather disagreements with grace? Teach me what it means to truly love the family you've surrounded me with. May I put 1 Corinthians 13 into practice today, surrendering my need to have my own way. Teach me patience and kindness. Help me rejoice when things go well for my family. Teach me to speak the truth in love, I pray. Amen.

Day Twenty-Five: I Surrender My Habits

To know me is to realize I'm a list maker. And when all those habit books started popping up in bookstores, I consumed them, making habit trackers and filling in empty dots. So when I created this piece, I ripped the habits from the headlines of my life. I still don't drink water very well! We all struggle with the discipline of habits.

The apostle Paul uses a training metaphor to encourage the Corinthian believers toward habitual discipline.

> Don't you realize that in a race everyone runs, but only one person gets the prize? So run to win! All athletes are disciplined in their training. They do it to win a prize that will fade away, but we do it for an eternal prize. So I run with purpose in every step. I am not just shadowboxing. I discipline my body like an athlete, training it to do what it should. Otherwise, I fear that after preaching to others I myself might be disqualified. (1 Corinthians 9:24-27)

The soles of our feet hit the road of our daily lives. Where we walk, talk, live, and move is the crux of who we are. Those little habits pepper our souls and bring solace or worry. We don't have to live reactive lives, simply responding to what happens around us. We can choose intentionality. We can invite God into the mundane, welcoming him into life's messiness. Daily surrender looks an awful lot like an ongoing conversation with God about big things and little.

To surrender your daily (bad) habits is to first recognize them as detrimental to your overall mental, spiritual, social, and physical health. Take an inventory today. What small actions (if continually practiced over time) will negatively affect you? Here are some ideas:

- having a cocktail every day
- jumping to judgment first without slowing down to hear the whole story
- running ragged until you fall into bed exhausted
- giving in to pessimism
- avoiding people as a rule
- binging on entertainment
- overeating past satiety

- escaping from all conflict
- telling "little" lies to avoid conflict
- saying yes to everything, even when you'd rather say no
- taking time for everyone else except yourself
- hollering at drivers in other cars
- staying up late
- procrastinating
- retreating indoors rather than going outside
- blaming others for your own issues
- hoarding
- giving in to chaos or disorganization
- overthinking and ruminating

The beauty of surrendering bad habits means you have the chance to fill the vacuum with something good. As you do so, you not only rid yourself of those toxic practices, but typically you add something beneficial to fill the space. What a powerful practice for daily living!

Jesus, I surrender my habits to you. I realize I don't always practice those little steps that help me grow closer to you. Help me take an accurate inventory of what I've done that is harming me so that I can ask you to empower me to enact new, positive, God-honoring rituals. I don't want to do this in my own strength. I understand you love me no matter what my habit landscape looks like. But I do pray that I would love myself as you do, so much so that I want to take care of me. Thank you that little by little is more powerful than gigantic gestures. I'm reminded of your words about being faithful in little things. Help me to do that today. Amen.

Day Twenty-Six: I Surrender My Appearance

Flowers are beautiful, but their petals fall off and their glory fades. When I look at today's handsomeness/beauty standards, I can grow discouraged at the places I do not measure up. I may compare myself with someone else's bouquet, forgetting the uniqueness of my own. Have you ever felt that way? I love how clarifying God's words to Samuel are—we are to look inward rather than outward. "Don't judge by his appearance or height, for I have rejected him. The LORD doesn't see things the way you see them. People judge by outward appearance, but the LORD looks at the heart" (1 Samuel 16:7).

In 1 Samuel 16, when Samuel was tasked with uncovering who the next king of Israel would be, Jesse's boys were paraded before him. While many looked kingly, the Lord had not chosen any of them. It's only when David, the runt, was pulled in from the sheepfolds that Samuel laid eyes on the king. These words are what the Lord reminded Samuel—that he doesn't consider beauty to come from appearances, but from the heart.

We see this in Jesus' constant teaching about the importance of our hearts. He said, "It's not what goes into your body that defiles you; you are defiled by what comes from your heart" (Mark 7:15). If we want to truly be attractive to others or feel better about how we look, we must shift away from the siren call of social media's ideas of outward appearance and, instead, turn the mirror on our hearts because they are the seat of beauty and handsomeness.

We always have the opportunity to grow a beautiful soul, to move from glory to glory, from grace to grace. We can become more forgiving, more patient, more openhearted. With the help of the Spirit within us, we can grow and bear fruit.

It's normal to struggle with aging, body image, or not fitting into society's oft restrictive (and ever changing) appearance standards. There is grief that comes from being left out, overlooked, or not "up to par." But as we meditate on the Scripture about Samuel, we realize there's an entirely different set of standards for the person who loves the Lord—it's a focus turned toward cultivating an internal beauty, a heart that beats like Jesus'.

That kind of beauty comes from the way we love others, how we welcome new relationships, or the manner in which we worship the One who fashioned us in our mother's wombs. A beautiful soul cannot be quickly manufactured or painted over; it must be part of a slow and steady obedience throughout our lives. Often our growth comes, too, in the crucible of relationships, not in the silo of isolation. In short—other people and their influence on our lives help us have beautiful souls.

Jesus, I surrender my appearance to you. I give you my struggle with body image, external validation, and the world's well-shouted definitions of worth. Instead, replace those worldly scripts with your encouragement. Remind me afresh that you look at the heart, not at outward appearance. Help me value those things as well. Lord, I want to be more and more attractive in my soul each year. Deliver me from the lie that I equal how I look. Instead, keep me closer and closer to you so my soul prospers and beautifies. No matter who I encounter, train me to value them based on their character rather than their appearance. Amen.

Day Twenty-Seven: I Surrender That Particular Outcome

I painted a bull's eye for this piece because it reveals our myopic view of what we want to happen. We pine for one outcome, forgetting the rest of the target is wide and allows for different "hits." And sometimes life hits us outside the target, yet we find the unexpected to still be a place of goodness.

We can rest in knowing God perfectly understands the best outcomes for our lives. Paul teaches, “And I am certain that God, who began the good work within you, will continue his work until it is finally finished on the day when Christ Jesus returns” (Philippians 1:6). He best knows how to hold us, even when things don’t turn out the way we anticipated.

It’s not hard to fixate on one particular thing we would like to see happen. We may feel our lives would be better if only we got that specific job. Or we’d feel less anxious if a difficult relationship resolved. Or maybe we think we’d be truly fulfilled if that ministry opportunity opened up. With anxiety reigning, it’s no wonder we believe if that one conundrum was solved, our lives would sing. And yet, our minds naively hang our hopes on an outcome, and we forget that God is working in and through every circumstance, even when things don’t go the way we wanted or planned.

During this season of surrender, we’re working on letting go. But surrendering that thing you most want in the world is one of the most difficult acts of laying something down. Often when we solely place our hopes on an outcome, it reveals that idolatry is in play.

So, see this moment as an opportunity for God to search your heart. Ask yourself these questions to discern the deeper meaning of your longing:

- Why do I need this thing/event/decision to happen?
- What do I gain if this comes to pass?
- What do I lose if this happens?
- How does my relationship with God intersect this desire?
- How can I be faithful if this dream dies?

- What am I learning about myself and my prayer life through this longing?
- Have I left room for a creative solution?
- Will I be angry if this outcome doesn't come to pass? Why or why not?
- How will this current situation (that doesn't meet my expectations) empower me to help others on a similar journey?
- How would a mature Christ follower work through this desire?

It's normal to have longings. It's common to desire one thing to come to pass, particularly if it seems to be a linchpin of our happiness. Even if outcomes don't turn out, our God is still worthy, faithful, and kind.

Jesus, I surrender that particular outcome to you. Show me if I've been pining after it, praying for it, or longing for it to happen so much that I've forgotten you. Forgive me if I have replaced you with a favorable circumstance, hoping that if it just comes true, I'll finally be happy. Instead, I surrender the entire situation to you, and I choose to find joy no matter what outcome happens. Teach me contentment and trust as I wait. I lay the whole situation before you. I take my hands off. Amen.

Day Twenty-Eight: I Surrender My Finances

Any wealth we receive is sheer gift. God often reminds us that we are the stewards of what he has given us. He has it all—we are simply managers. So I created a wallet with flowers to remind me of the gifts he's given, that they're a bouquet meant to be held loosely or given away. The author of Hebrews reminds us that a fixation on money causes deep dissatisfaction in our lives. "Don't love money; be satisfied with what you have. For God has said, 'I will never fail you. I will never abandon you'" (Hebrews 13:5). Our Father loves to provide for our needs.

Our faith in Christ is deeply tied to our management of finances. The way we spend our money reflects our priorities, passions, and purpose. And when we worry about provision, we reveal that we're shrinking away from trusting God.

Jesus reminds his disciples in the Sermon on the Mount that he will provide for those whose hearts bend toward his. He said, "Seek the Kingdom of God above all else, and live righteously, and he will give you everything you need" (Matthew 6:33). His words hint at empire, particularly God's kingdom.

When we are consumed with our own empire, fretting enters in.

But when we are dazzled by God's kingdom and live for nonmonetary outcomes, *shalom* reigns.

That doesn't negate the fact that we live in a world centered on commerce and money. Nor does it silence the wooing of social media that constantly reminds us we don't have enough. The truth is every human being struggles with provision. We all fret about not having enough.

So to surrender this part of you is an important part of your discipleship journey with Jesus. It reveals that you are more interested in trusting him than in finagling your life to get more. The pathway of surrender involves the art of contentment—not an easy spiritual practice for a world swimming in malcontent.

Like the Israelite people who often forgot about the provision of God, we tend toward forgetfulness too. To remember God's faithfulness is to retrain our minds toward belief. God is sovereign. He owns it all. He knows how to provide for birds, flowers, and this earth. Surely, he knows how to take care of his children. Thanking him for past provision is a good first step in surrendering your current financial situation to him.

Jesus, I surrender my finances to you. I choose to trust you to provide, but I often see how I forget about all your past provisions. Instead of that, help me recount the many times you've been faithful to me. You do own everything, and I am simply a steward of those resources. Help me to manage what I have—for your glory and your kingdom. Curb my greed. Curtail my spending. Help me realize afresh that things and money are not going to satisfy my soul. I choose contentment today, Jesus, as I trust you to lead me in this difficult area of my life. Amen.

Day Twenty-Nine: I Surrender the World's Wisdom

It's simplistic, I know, to use a lightbulb to connote wisdom, but hear me out. In this case, the light is the world's intelligence, but it does not illuminate in this painting. The closer you get to this artificial light, the darker it grows. We may think the world offers us insight, but only the true Light reveals the truth and guides us well. God's wisdom yields a changed life. James writes, "But the wisdom from above is first of all pure. It is also peace loving, gentle at all times, and willing to yield to others. It is full of mercy and the fruit of good deeds. It shows no favoritism and is always sincere" (James 3:17).

We are saturated by the wisdom of the world. It permeates us like a Texas rainstorm in May. It is the atmosphere we breathe. The difficult thing about worldly wisdom is it sounds so logical, so easy to follow.

If we spend all our time in this world and don't pull away to seek God's wisdom, our decisions will be based on a false premise whose center is this: me. When we make choices based solely on our desires and what we perceive will make us happy, we are forsaking the deeper wisdom of serving others.

James highlights this idea as he describes godly wisdom in 3:17. It mirrors Jesus Christ who held all these traits—purity, peace, a yielding spirit, mercy, goodness, fairness, and sincerity. But those traits are not heralded by the powers that be. To uncover the world's way of doing things, consider the opposite of these traits—impurity, discord, walking over others, wickedness, unfairness, and being disingenuous.

To surrender the world's wisdom is to recognize that we do not have all the answers in our limited resources. We cannot access the intelligence of the universe through our own minds. There is humility in recognizing our limitations. And when we let go of the popular advice *du jour*, we leave space to be transformed in our minds through the Word of God.

To discover the kind of wisdom that empowers us to love others well and be agents of healing in God's kingdom, we can mine it in the Bible's pages, particularly in the book of Proverbs. If you're lacking wisdom during this forty-day journey, consider picking up that wisdom book and reading a chapter or two a day. God's wisdom is readily available to us.

Earlier in James, we read that God delights to give us this kind of wisdom. "If you need wisdom, ask our generous God, and he will give it to you. He will not rebuke you for asking" (James 1:5). What he shares with you will be counterintuitive to the world's way of doing things, but if you heed it, peace and growth await.

Jesus, I surrender the world's wisdom to you. Forgive me for chasing after it, believing it to be the pathway to success and popularity. You remind me to transform my mind through your Word. Help me be so immersed in your Word that I can easily recognize the voice of the world. Renew my mind. Forgive me for capitulating to the world's wisdom just so I won't be persecuted or called out. Give me boldness for the things of you and empower me to follow you no matter how unpopular your way may be. I love you more than the world's way of doing things! Amen.

Day Thirty: I Surrender My Job

I painted a mug on my desk to remind us of our jobs. We all have differing professions, but perhaps we all use pens at some point, even if we mow lawns for a living. All of us have tools of the trade, and as a writer and artist, pens are mine. I find I even need to relinquish control of the way I use my tools every day, seeking God for new ways to do things and fresh ways to approach my job. I've often loved Colossians 3:23-24 when I think about my work: "Work willingly at whatever you do, as though you were working for the Lord rather than for people. Remember that the Lord will give you an inheritance as your reward, and that the Master you are serving is Christ."

Colossians 3:23-24 reverberated through me in one of my first jobs in college. As a pantry chef, I wanted to honor my employers in how I served and created desserts and salads. There were times, however, that the lure of strawberries got the best of me, and I ate a few. It was these verses I had memorized that began to haunt me, and I confessed my strawberry stealing to my boss.

Integrity in the workplace matters—not because it helps us advance in our careers, but because being honest and forthright are traits that reveal our relationship with Jesus. Jobs occupy (word intended!) most of our waking lives, so surrendering them is an important spiritual discipline. There are many ways to lay down our jobs for the glory of Jesus:

- We surrender when our jobs don't fulfill us.
- We surrender when our salary doesn't meet our needs and wants.
- We surrender when we're ill-treated and unseen.
- We surrender when we're overlooked for a promotion.
- We surrender when someone who cheats gets ahead of us.
- We surrender when there are other jobs we'd rather have.
- We surrender when our boss doesn't understand us.
- We surrender when we worry that we'll lose our job.
- We surrender when our position is eliminated.
- We surrender when we feel lackadaisical about our employment.
- We surrender when we have conflicts at work.
- We surrender when our workplace produces anxiety.
- We surrender when we love our job.

- We surrender when we despise our daily work.
- We surrender when we are the only one who knows we've done a good job.
- We surrender when we didn't get that raise.
- We surrender when the pension fund diminishes.
- We surrender when our job doesn't reflect our passion.

To surrender is to set aside control, to lay all our workplace anxieties at the feet of the One whom we work for. According to today's verse, we don't work for human beings per se, we work for Jesus. And he is an amazing boss!

Jesus, I surrender my job to you. There are times when it energizes me, but there are also times my job breeds frustration. I give my tasks to you. I surrender my fatigue. Help me to honor you during my work. Enable me to love others well in this position you've given me. Remind me afresh of what it means to build the kingdom in the midst of my occupation. I choose to work hard, honor you, be honest, and rest in the outcomes. Give me your insight into my next steps, I pray. Amen.

Day Thirty-One: I Surrender My Gifts

This is such a simple piece, and I almost hesitated to draw it, but I envisioned a ribbon with gift tags. Each of our lives is one long grosgrain of lifespan, and we are gifted along the way to meet the needs of others and live our adventure well. Gifts are unique, accessible, and available, as Paul points out in 1 Corinthians 12:4-6: "There are different kinds of spiritual gifts, but the same Spirit is the source of them all. There are different kinds of service, but we serve the same Lord. God works in different ways, but it is the same God who does the work in all of us." The variety of gifts we all possess is an indication of the creativity of our Creator.

What a beautiful surprise that God not only saves us from the ravages of sin and death, but he graces us with gifts. Each one of us has been given spiritual gifts—not merely for our enjoyment but for the betterment of others. And yet? There is so much joy when we operate within our unique God-given shape.

God gives good gifts, and his creative power means he imbues each of us with a unique giftedness. When we look at Jesus' many parables about money, talents, and vineyards, we see how important it is to use our gifts for the sake of his kingdom—in service of others. In Matthew 25:31-46 Jesus talks about a reckoning at the end of time, where people will be rewarded because of how they used their unique abilities to meet the needs of many.

When he speaks of reward, the people who served were perplexed. "Then these righteous ones will reply, 'Lord, when did we ever see you hungry and feed you? Or thirsty and give you something to drink? Or a stranger and show you hospitality? Or naked and give you clothing? When did we ever see you sick or in prison and visit you?' And the King will say, 'I tell you the truth, when you did it to one of the least of these my brothers and sisters, you were doing it to me!'" (Matthew 25:37-40). When we exercise our gifts, we demonstrate our love for Jesus.

Gifts are meant to be given, not hoarded. Our joyful act of worship is to surrender them for the sake of the kingdom. It's to view them openhandedly, in anticipation for the next adventure of service God has for you.

And as God gives you strength, spend it joyfully for others—and in that, you will experience the abundant life he has planned for you.

Jesus, I surrender my gifts to you. Thank you for them. Thank you for making me uniquely me. I don't want to bury the gifts you've given me in a field. Instead, I want to hear "Well done, good and faithful servant" one day. So spur me on to action. Help me receive those gifts with joy, choosing not to compare them with other people's abilities. Give me contentment in the talents you've given me. May I understand the privilege it is to serve you! I want to honor you with everything inside me. I want to see your kingdom built in my little locale. I want to spend my life for your sake. Thank you for entrusting me with these gifts, Lord. Help me to use them joyfully for you. Amen.

Day Thirty-Two: I Surrender My Way of Doing Things

My own way of doing things (though I often think they're right) has often become a cage of my own making. When I'm rigid in my practice, I don't tend to branch out, and I certainly don't trust God because I can trust my tried-and-true methods. So I painted a bird cage where the happy yellow bird breaks free from the cage in order to soar. May it be that we can perceive the freedom that comes from letting go of our way of doing things.

In the book of Judges, we see the outworking of those who kept choosing what they felt was right. There, you see wars, conflicts, death, and endless cycles of sin, repentance, then sin again. These words are haunting: "In those days Israel had no king; all the people did whatever seemed right in their own eyes" (Judges 17:6).

The world holds such shallow "wisdom." It reminds us to take shortcuts, satiate our own base desires, and look out for ourselves only. It promises a quick fix, a short-term solution to a complicated problem, or entices us with escape.

Sometimes we can fetishize our way of doing things, as if our methods are sacred and any other way of seeing a situation or accomplishing tasks is wrong. Problem is, we live in a complex world, and there are often many nuanced ways God leads his people toward their next steps. If we worship our way, we tend to think poorly of any other way, and we remain closed to the growth God has for us in those uncomfortable places.

Change is hard. And in a whirlwind of chaos, we tend to cling to what is known, what we've felt to be comfortable. Like Peter walking on the water toward Jesus (see Matthew 14:22-33), defying the laws of gravity, God calls us away from our way of doing things into a life of faith where there is the very real possibility of failure. Thankfully, in that unstable place of trusting God, he holds and sustains us.

When we are staid in our methods of trust, often Jesus will shake the waves around us so that we realize everything we've trusted in is unsteady. Only he is worthy of our deepest trust. Only his way is the path toward a life of faith. And when we begin to sink, and all else feels lost, the strong arm of Christ reaches through the waves to rescue us.

It's easy to fall back on doing what is right in our own eyes. To surrender our way of doing things is to humble ourselves, recognizing we don't have all the answers. As we surrender, we become more tender toward others who see the world differently than we do—doing so leaves space for compassion and empathy.

Jesus, I surrender my way of doing things to you. Why do I feel my way is best? I'm sure there's pride lurking inside me. Root it out, Lord. Forgive me for judging others when they don't conform to my prescription for their lives. Forgive me for erring on the side of judgment rather than love. Forgive me for worshiping my way. Your way is best. Love is best. Giving up control means you can do your best work. Empower me today to let go of needing everything to be done my way. Instead, Lord, I choose to rest in your beautiful ways. Amen.

Day Thirty-Three: I Surrender My Reputation

I don't know about you, but I have spent a lot of time trying to manage my reputation. I've wanted my narration of events to prevail over others, proving my rightness. That's why I painted a megaphone (oh it's loud) as a symbol of that struggle. However, when I've learned to surrender and let the Lord defend me, his defense is far better—it's nuanced, scented, and sweet.

We worry about many things, particularly because worry is the oxygen of our world. Worry indicates we're exercising our fretting muscle, even though we know life is much better when we're living with trust and faith. Oswald Chambers wrote this in his famous devotional *My Utmost for His Highest:* "God is my Father, He loves me, I shall never think of anything He will forget. Why should I worry?" Why indeed?

Reputation is one of those worries.

Peter reminds us of the importance of our reputation, that our outsides should match what Jesus has done on the inside—and our actions should be a signpost to our friends and neighbors. "Be careful to live properly among your unbelieving neighbors. Then even if they accuse you of doing wrong, they will see your honorable behavior, and they will give honor to God when he judges the world" (1 Peter 2:12). It's quite simple: to have a good reputation is to act reputably.

Even when we do live honorably, we still cannot control what other people think about us. We *can* control who we are, how we interact with others, and we *can* pursue authenticity. But if someone maligns us wrongly, what should we do?

The answer isn't so simple. It might be right in some situations to speak the truth in love and share the truth to clear the air. In other instances, God may call us to the discipline of silence, allowing our reputation to be marred (and letting God do our PR).

This is why it's important to spend time listening to the Holy Spirit—because he knows exactly what is necessary in the moment. When you are maligned, your knee-jerk reaction may be to defend, but the Spirit may hold you back. Or he may nudge you toward disclosure.

Either way, our beautiful act of surrender is deeply connected to our character, which is expressed in today's Scripture.

No matter what our reputation, our aim should be to hold firmly to the One whose reputation was marred, maligned, and lied about. Friend, he understands when you walk a similar path. He knows how to intercede for you and defend you. He loves you so much, and, in return, he simply asks for your surrender.

Jesus, I surrender my reputation to you, particularly when it's maligned. I know it's not my job to do frenetic reputation management, but so often I jump into that role. Help me be silent. Hold my tongue. Bring me to a mature place where I truly entrust my reputation to you. You are so capable of defending me, so I trust you today to do so. Help me no longer run around hoping to make everyone like me. It's exhausting, so I truly, truly surrender my reputation to you. Protect me, I pray. Show me when to speak up and when to stay silent, I pray. Amen.

Day Thirty-Four: I Surrender My Expectations

We all have expectations of God. As I thought about that, my mind shifted to the middle part of Isaiah 45:9: "Does a clay pot argue with its maker? Does the clay dispute with the one who shapes it, saying, 'Stop, you're doing it wrong!'" So I painted God as potter, hands coming from the heavens, shaping a clay vessel. We are that vessel, and although we may not appreciate the twists and turns our story takes, we must remember God, as our potter, gets to shape our stories.

This verse has brought comfort amid my great expectations: "You will be rewarded for this; your hope will not be disappointed" (Proverbs 23:18). But what happens when our expectations of God (or the way he answers our prayers) do not turn out the way we hope them to?

Expectations are gnarly creatures, difficult to tame, particularly when we place them on God. They take on a life of their own, haunting us, causing us to want-want-want what we don't yet have. Or they poison our moods when anything less comes to fruition, particularly in long-term prayers.

We can manage expectations by studying, then practicing, biblical hope. The proverb above hints at this, that as we exercise biblical hope, we will experience satisfaction. That kind of hope is based on the finished work of Jesus Christ—that invites us into a relationship with the Father who loves us and the Spirit who daily shapes us, even when what we pray for doesn't yet come to pass.

Hope cannot change; it does not waiver—even if God does not show up for us in what we perceive to be a timely manner. Hope does not shimmy under our expectations of God.

Somewhere in the middle is a sweet spot of expectations—to verbalize our longings to God through prayer, yet to let go of the outcomes, allowing our creative God to answer in a surprising way. It is to live openhanded and expectant: *God, I would love to see something new in that frustrating area of life, but if it does not come to pass, give me the endurance necessary to wait for another outcome. I give you permission to be creative in answering the cry of my heart.*

As you surrender your expectations of God today, consider that he holds the whole universe together. He knows your story from beginning to end, and he is working behind the scenes for your good and his glory. Though it feels impossible as you wait, it is a hallmark of a growing Christ follower to practice the fruit of patience.

God has good plans for you. He may not meet your expectations, particularly in your prescribed timing. But he is good, and his love cannot be revoked. He will not leave you. He will not walk away. What does he promise when your expectations are dashed? His presence that will always go with you, no matter what you face. You are not alone.

Jesus, I surrender my expectations to you. So often I am sad when my prayers aren't answered the way I want them to be, and when that happens, instead of turning to you, I sometimes blame you. I'm sorry if I've placed more hope in answers to prayer than I have in your steady character and your perfect timing. That certainly leaves very little room for you to surprise me with your presence and the unique plan you have for my life. Surprise me as I pray and wait for you this week. Help me surrender what I think should happen. Amen.

Day Thirty-Five: I Surrender Growing Older

I decided to paint a leaf from spring to summer to autumn to winter to symbolize our lives here on earth. Each season is important in the life cycle of a tree's leaves, yet society tells us we are only useful in spring when buds bloom or summer when fruit emerges. But so much happens in the remaining seasons, and each one is important, which is why I painted all seasons on one leaf.

The apostle Paul speaks to our human condition. Every day we are growing older, but each moment we can grow our souls. He writes:

> That is why we never give up. Though our bodies are dying, our spirits are being renewed every day. For our present troubles are small and won't last very long. Yet they produce for us a glory that vastly outweighs them and will last forever! So we don't look at the troubles we can see now; rather, we fix our gaze on things that cannot be seen. For the things we see now will soon be gone, but the things we cannot see will last forever. (2 Corinthians 4:16-18)

We are called to cultivate the unseen, the imperishable.

Every day we have the potential to grow glory, the kind of glory that reaches beyond the grave. But our world mitigates against this task, telling us that each year we celebrate a birthday, the less we have time to do all that we want to do.

Thankfully we have a choice every day. We can find Jesus in the margins of living our lives, settling into the beautiful potential of a soul constantly unfolding—that reaches heavenward and serves those God has entrusted to us. We always can grow closer to Jesus.

The problem comes when we try to retrofit our life on earth with the expectations of heaven. Earth can never satisfy a soul because our souls were meant for an entirely different realm. In *The Weight of Glory*, C. S. Lewis reminds us, "We are half-hearted creatures, fooling about with drink and sex and ambition when infinite joy is offered us, like an ignorant child who wants to go on making mud pies in a slum because he cannot imagine what is meant by the offer of a holiday at the sea. We are far too easily pleased."

To age is to grow closer to the person and place we were intended for. The holiday at sea beckons. We must shift our focus from the here and now (and the aches and pains therein) and, instead, look beyond, remembering that it's our faithfulness here that brings the weight of glory into the realm of the eternal.

Jesus, I surrender growing older to you. Every day I'm older, but this world prefers youthfulness and vigor, so I feel unseen and a bit panicked. Free me from the world's idea of worth. Instead, help me to use my own fear about growing older to be empathetic toward others. Help me dignify and really see other people who are older than me. Help me ask advice, listen well, and learn from them. My hope is that every year of my life I am growing closer and closer to you. Amen.

Day Thirty-Six: I Surrender My Health

The seat of our health is our heart, so I decided to embellish a heart with flowers and beauty and brightness. In painting a heart, I meant it for two dimensions—our physicality and our emotional health. Jesus often spoke to people about their hearts, that if our heart is off, our messaging and lives will be off. Oh, to have health from the inside out!

When our health is assaulted, or our bodies don't do what we want them to do, our tendency is to either research everything on Dr. Google and try to fix what ails us or, if the condition happens chronically, to slip into apathy and sadness. When we struggle with health issues, insecurities are exposed, worries heighten, and fear threatens.

With stressful health situations, we realize just how little is under our control.

Paul reminds us that we are God's dwelling place, so it matters how we live our lives in our bodies. "Don't you realize that your body is the temple of the Holy Spirit, who lives in you and was given to you by God? You do not belong to yourself, for God bought you with a high price. So you must honor God with your body" (1 Corinthians 6:19-20). But how?

Yes, we are God's temple. Our bodies house the very presence of the Holy Spirit. We are tasked with taking care of (stewarding) what God has given us. But what happens when our focus either shifts into hyper maintenance bordering on obsession, or we give up entirely? How can surrender help us?

Having an eschatological mindset does empower us, and today's Scripture hints at that. We are not merely bodies moving throughout earth, but we are precious carriers of God's presence wherever we go. One day these decaying bodies will be gloriously raised to new life—there will be no more pain, unhealth, or disorders. Our minds, bodies, and souls will be completely whole, vibrantly alive.

Today may be full of pains and unknowns. We may grow weary of the fight. A chronic condition wears on us and we wonder how much we must endure. These are all legitimate feelings. And when we feel saddened by the state of our health, we can find solace in remembering that Jesus, God in the flesh, enfleshed himself in a body. He experienced wounds and piercing and suffocation. He knows what it is like to feel physical, mental, and emotional pain. He endured all of that for our sakes. He understands. He empathizes. He weeps alongside.

Friend, you are not alone in your health struggle. Nor is your friend or neighbor or relative. You are seen. You are valued. You are not forgotten.

Jesus, I surrender my health to you. I don't understand everything about how my body is functioning or dysfunctioning, but you do. Help me to know the best pathway forward. Direct me to the right resources and professionals so I can get to the bottom of this. For those in my life who are suffering in their health, empower me to love them well, bringing much-needed empathy and direct care. Thank you that in the new heavens and the new earth my body will be whole and wholly alive. But in this in-between time, as I wait between the now and the not yet, give me the stamina to worship you in the way I steward my body. Amen.

Day Thirty-Seven: I Surrender My Agenda

I use clipboards in my life—quite often actually. I have weekly, monthly, and yearly goals, and I manage them with extensive lists. It is not easy for me to surrender my agenda, even daily. Still, I wanted to highlight the beauty surrounding the clipboard. Our lives become more "flowered" outside the to-do list; don't you think?

We read about God knowing the plans for us in Jeremiah 29, but have you considered what is written prior to that famous passage? "This is what the LORD of Heaven's Armies, the God of Israel, says to all the captives he has exiled to Babylon from Jerusalem: 'Build homes, and plan to stay. Plant gardens, and eat the food they produce. Marry and have children. Then find spouses for them so that you may have many grandchildren. Multiply! Do not dwindle away! And work for the peace and prosperity of the city where I sent you into exile. Pray to the LORD for it, for its welfare will determine your welfare'" (Jeremiah 29:4-7). We tend to fret over grandiose future plans while forgetting the mundane.

God's aim is for us to thrive amid our own Babylon. We, too, are exiles on this earth, just like the Israelites were during the time of exile to Babylon. To thrive means to do the next right thing. Serve our families. Work with all our might (as God gives us strength). Feed others. Pursue relationships. Enlarge our territories and influence. Seek peace. Pray. Be a light in darkness.

While it's normal to worry about next steps, don't let that fretting prevent you from living for Jesus today in your present circumstances.

To surrender your agenda, besides seeking to thrive where you are, is to ask God to help you become interruptible. During tasks upon tasks, we tend to elevate our current agenda over the needs of the people in our lives.

Does this mean that if we surrender our agendas to the Lord that all will be well? Again, remember the context of Jeremiah—the nation of Israel lived in the pain of exile, which was certainly not their desire. Jesus promised us, "I have told you all this so that you may have peace in me. Here on earth you will have many trials and sorrows. But take heart, because I have overcome the world" (John 16:33). Trials and sorrows are a normative part of the Christ-following life, but he doesn't end with that—he finishes his realism with hope: a reminder to take heart.

His aim is your thriving—even if you're facing a difficult time today.

Jesus, I surrender my agenda to you. I really want to succeed, but I also know in longing for that, I could take my eyes off your plan for me. Forgive me when I've pursued my lists more than I've asked you for direction and help. Thank you that I may have many plans, but your purpose will prevail, even when I'm hurting or life is painful. There is freedom and peace in knowing that you will help me when things fall apart. Teach me the art of thriving where I am. I choose to trust you with all my heart, and instead of relying on my understanding of a situation, I choose to acknowledge you in everything I do. You are the planner; I am the plan-ee. Help me rest in that. Amen.

Day Thirty-Eight: I Surrender My Burnout

It is obvious, perhaps, that I would choose the imagery of a fire to illustrate burnout, but it just made sense to me. When you gaze at a fire as it dies, what is left are embers, then ash. All that wood is no more. So it is for us. We can only burn for so long. Unless we keep adding fuel, we'll burn clear out.

A few years ago I had to take a sabbatical for the sake of my mental health. I had not only brushed up against burnout, but I was on the verge of a collapse. Part of retreating meant looking backward to all the ways I tried to handle the difficulties of life solely on my own—not with God's strength, nor with the counsel of others.

In burnout, I tell myself to return to Paul's prayer for the Colossians. "We also pray that you will be strengthened with all his glorious power so you will have all the endurance and patience you need. May you be filled with joy, always thanking the Father. He has enabled you to share in the inheritance that belongs to his people, who live in the light" (Colossians 1:11-12). Oh, to access that kind of joyful endurance when I'm tired!

We live in a rushed and complicated world with expectations multiplied through square-shaped posts and evocative videos on our phone screens. Whereas years ago we learned about other opportunities through print magazines and newspapers—something we could take or leave—social media now shouts at us about our incapability from our phones, and it parades all sorts of options we could or should be doing to have that elusive "best life now."

It's exhausting.

Couple that with the need to make a living, and we face the kind of pressures no society has ever faced. No wonder we're on the brink of burnout. So what are we to do?

In surrendering our burnout, we take note of our capacities. We are not omnipotent, more powerful than wind and sky and stars, but God is. We cannot be omnipresent, in every place at every time, but God is. We are not omniscient, knowing all mysteries, but God is. Surrender means simply acknowledging that he is God, and we are not.

Those limitations, while frustrating, can become doorways of hope. The good news is that Christianity isn't about us doing a bunch of tasks until we burn out for Jesus. Instead, it's a recognition of our need, married to his capabilities.

Whether you have been burned out, you currently are over-tasked, or you approach a season of busyness, the Lord carries it all—past, present, and future. This is good news, indeed.

Jesus, I surrender burnout to you. All that rush and worry has me completely exhausted. Forgive me for not obeying your call to sabbath rest. I live as if everything is up to me, and I can't seem to stop and let go. Resting is an act of faith, but burnout reveals I am relying on my own strength. I want to have holy rhythms in my life. I want to take strategic and necessary breaks to refuel and remind myself that I am far more than what I do. Thank you for modeling rest when you walked the earth, Jesus. Since I want to be your dedicated follower, I choose, too, to rest and trust you for provision when I stop striving. Amen.

Day Thirty-Nine: I Surrender My Ministry

I know that not all ministry happens inside the four walls of a church, but this was the image that first came to mind. In painting this, I'm aware of the pain that many have experienced in Christian contexts, whether as leaders or participants. The church is simply a called-out people, practicing sacraments and striving to love well. But ministry is full of humans, and pain happens. I painted the door red to remind us that we all need the blood of Jesus, particularly as we serve him.

Every Christ follower has a ministry. That position may not be paid; it may not be glamorous (love seldom is, actually); it may not be recognized as such. But the truth is we are all tasked with the Great Commission—to make disciples in our context, remembering that this work is alongside the work of Christ. It is of great comfort that he will never leave us—particularly in ministry. (See Matthew 28:19-20.)

Unfortunately, there seems to be a hierarchical understanding of ministry, as if there's a heavenly org chart where the pastor reigns on the top, followed by the missionary, then perhaps the worship leader. These up-front "ministries" sometimes make us feel like what we do in the margins of life is not official. But what we do, no matter how small, matters. Loving, discipling, caring, listening—this is all the work of the disciple of Christ.

Often, we look forward as we think of potential ministry plans. While it's good to dream, we may neglect the weightier matters of ministry right in front of us. Our calling is to the people in our lives—and this is often unapplauded.

So to surrender our ministry means to surrender our idea of what ministry looks like. This is why the apostle Paul talks often about different parts of the body performing different functions. Look at how he phrases it: "If the whole body were an eye, how would you hear? Or if your whole body were an ear, how would you smell anything? But our bodies have many parts, and God has put each part just where he wants it. How strange a body would be if it had only one part!" (1 Corinthians 12:17-19). Just because the work you do for the Lord looks differently than others, it is no less commendable. We all need each other; we all play our parts.

In surrendering, we realize that God has unique roles for us all. The mandate is the same—make disciples—but the way we do it differs wildly from person to person. As you surrender your role in the body of Christ, be expectant. God loves to surprise you with doors you never thought would open, and he is good about tying up loose ends to move you forward.

Jesus, I surrender my ministry. It's not mine; it's yours. Help me to hold it loosely, entrusting my heart and soul to you. Open doors for me to serve you in unexpected and unacknowledged ways. Remind me that ministry is not about a stage but about receptiveness to your Spirit within me. Keep me close to you so I can hear your still, small voice on behalf of those I pray for, serve, and love. Empower me to make disciples in my everyday life and to see dignity in that. I want to shepherd well the people you've placed in my life. Thank you for giving me such a good example of service, Jesus. Amen.

Day Forty: I Surrender My Future

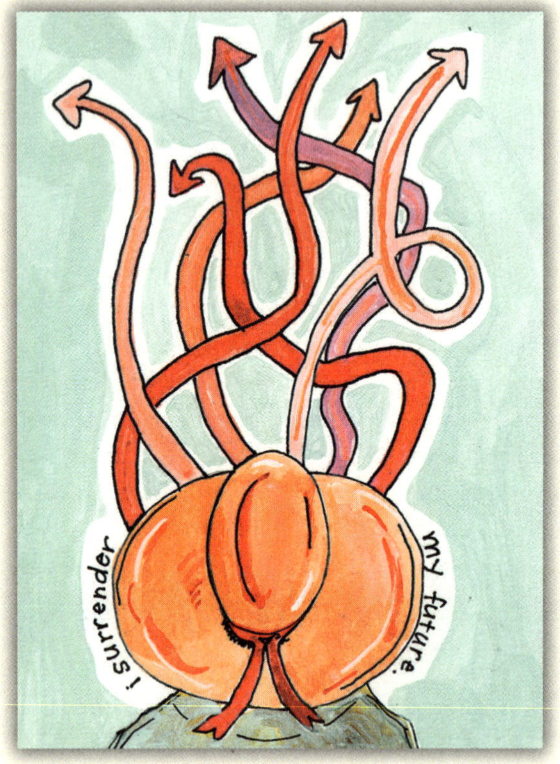

There are so many ways our futures could turn and twist, so I decided to create a hatted person looking toward the future with Medusa-like pathways to indicate just how odd it is that we pre-judge and predict the future. We simply cannot know the pathway ahead of us.

The future looms. It is unseen, pristine, and it beckons. Peter assures us of this future when he encourages, "All praise to God, the Father of our Lord Jesus Christ. It is by his great mercy that we have been born again, because God raised Jesus Christ from the dead. Now we live with great expectation, and we have a priceless inheritance—an inheritance that is kept in heaven for you, pure and undefiled, beyond the reach of change and decay" (1 Peter 1:3-4). Our future is assured. We have a guaranteed inheritance.

So why do we worry so much about the future?

According to the verse above, we can live with great expectation. For beyond the future of our earthly life lies an imperishable reward that cannot be removed by others. It is based on the finished work of the Lord through us. Moth and rust cannot destroy the reward. Time cannot erase it. The beautiful truth is this: we have a spiritual legacy that will follow us to eternity.

Surrendering gives us a purpose today, causing us to do work that follows us forward, makes a difference, and changes the landscape of the kingdom of God in our generation. What a beautiful task!

We cannot begin to comprehend the beauty that God will bring our way. But we can have good spiritual habits today. We can prepare our hearts by reading the Bible. We can reach out to the hurting, pray for the sick, and forgive that person that hurt us. We can live the Sermon on the Mount, following in the footsteps of Jesus in the strength he provides.

What we do today is a trickle of a stream. Each habit and prayer and surrender is another drop forming into a river of what's next. All of it matters. None of it is overlooked. And when we make mistakes or our hearts bend toward sin, we have a throne of grace to approach and a Savior who lives to intercede for us.

What is true of the future is true of today.

You are loved.

You are endowed with worth.

You are given work to do that has meaning.

You are forgiven.

You are made whole.

You are weak, yet strong.

You are sacrificed for.

You are set free.

You are alive.

You are wounded, yet healing.

You are held.

You are unique.

You are wanted.

You are lovely.

Rest in these present and future truths today, particularly as you surrender.

Jesus, I surrender my future to you. I am afraid. I don't know what will happen next, but I know that you do. Please replace my fretting with faith in your ability to take care of me. When my mind gets utterly preoccupied with what may happen, reorient my thinking toward your faithfulness and all the beautiful things you've done in my life. I want to concentrate on your goodness rather than stress about my future. Thank you that you hold my future in your capable, beautiful hands. Thank you that what is true of me today is true of me tomorrow. Thank you that my work will follow me forward to eternity. Amen.